# SAVED, SINGLE
# SISTER
## Real Talk

GODZCHILD PUBLICATIONS

Published by Godzchild Publications
a division of Godzchild, Inc.
22 Halleck St., Newark, NJ 07104
www.godzchildproductions.net

Printed in the United States of America 2012— First Edition
Cover Design by Ana Saunders of Es3lla Designs

Library of Congress Cataloging-in-Publications Data
Saved, Single Sister: Real Talk/Pamala Mintz

ISBN    978-1-937095-65-9 (pbk.)

1. Mintz, Pamala. 2. Fiction 3. Personal Growth 4. Spiritual Growth
4. Christianity 5. Women's Issues

# SSS – SAVED, SINGLE SISTER

## Chronicle 1

**CHARACTERS APRIL** *Divorced mother of 3*

**SHARON** *Adopted mother of 1*

**LISA** *No Kids*

**NICOLE** *Single mother of 3*

**SAVANNAH** *April's co-worker*

**TYRONE** *April's co-worker*

**ERIC JACKSON** *Banker   uncommitted man (online)*

**EDWARD WILLIAMS** *Mortician (family friend)*

**ROBERT** *April's ex-husband (Michael's father)*

**FRANKLIN** *April's older two baby daddy*

MARK JOSEPHS Older man – life insurance salesman
(met online)

*I am dedicating my first published writing to my mother, Paulette J. Mintz. As a single mother, she taught me the value of hard work. I love you, Mommy!*

# FOREWORD

*"A sister is a gift to the heart, a friend to the spirit, a golden thread to the meaning of life." - Isadora James*

*I*n life, people enter for different reasons; some for a season, some for the moment and some for the rest of your life. God has blessed me with them all during my forty something years of life. Who would have thought that in 1998 my friend and sister would walk into my life? I believe in my heart that God has placed her here as a "for the rest of my life" person.

During our years of friendship, I have watched you as a quiet single mother of three dealing with self-esteem issues trying to understand the God that we serve. Pam, you once told me you would never attend a Pentecostal church or catch that thing called the Holy Ghost that makes people act crazy and speak a funny language. You thought the Holy Ghost speaking, church people were all CRAZY! Notice the statement we were all crazy. Now all I can say is who's crazy now, Pam? HALLELUJAH!!!

Through the years, I have watched your spiritual life grow through leaps and bounds. One should never count a person out, but trust God and walk with them holding their hand if necessary. I must back go back to 1998. I never wanted to be Pam's friend, but God knew best. We actually needed each other; just as there was a Paul & Silas, Naomi & Ruth, David & Jonathan, Esther & her cousin Mordecai, God knows what we need in our life to push us, encourage and even tell us the truth, even when it hurts. My sister, you are chosen by God, regardless of not understanding every experience of your life that has caused you pain and grief. You have been chosen by God, even when the journey gets hard and the challenges have not been removed.

My friend, you have been chosen by God, even when you feel like you can't make it through your difficult days.

Yes, Pam, you are chosen by God when pain, sickness, and financial situations just don't seem to be getting any better.

We have learned through the years that when we put God first in every area of our life and when the enemy comes against us like a flood, the spirit of the Lord shall lift up a standard against him. Isaiah 59:19

It hasn't been easy being a sister and friend to Pamala Mintz, but we have learned to disagree in love. We are sisters to the end with God on our side.

Love You Much,
*Supreina Mason*

# INTRODUCTION

Saved, Single Sister is a realistic view of the daily lifestyles of Christian women and the reality of dating. Most women can relate to one or more of the characters in the book. Sit back, relax and enjoy the journey of four very different women that have one thing in common – their relationship with God.

# DISCLAIMER

The characters in this book are fictitious. You may relate to one or more of the characters in this book. My prayer is that not only do you relate to a character or two but also that true deliverance will come to the "lonely woman". If Steve Harvey can empower you to "think like a man," I know God can empower you to "think like the true woman" he created you to be. I am a believer that you can have wisdom to overcome obstacles, but that doesn't mean you need to change your character as the woman God created you to be. Knowledge is power. The women we crucify in the Bible are the women from which we should adapt the most characteristics.

How did I get here? I am almost 40 years old and I am still having "how did I get here" moments. "God help me!" Every year, I approach another birthday SINGLE! WHY?? Don't I deserve a husband? What did I do to have to wait? I know what I will do. I will find my own man. Yes, April, let's do this girl. But Lord knows I haven't done a good job up to this point. God, I love you but......

I am lonely and want companionship. I miss a man's touch. I miss a man's kisses. Darn it, I am tired of buying batteries. I want the real thing! What am I saying? Do I want sex? Yes, that will work! I can call one of my MMs. In case you didn't know, MM stands for married men. You know ... the ones who don't want commitment, but can hit that spot just right! But if one of them comes over, I will be left alone again after they leave. So do I want sex or a commitment? Sex sounds good right now but how will I ever get what God has for me if I.......... UGHHHHHH! What am I going to do? This emotional roller coaster is killing me. I can't tell anybody. They think I have it all together. I can't even tell my bestie. She won't understand either. God, you are my only outlet. I can't tell anybody I own a toy. I can't tell people I meet men online and most times it ends in just sex. I can't tell anyone I sleep with married men. Then there are the really nice young men, but then I will be categorized as a cougar. But the young men are putting it down! Whew!!! But are they "family" material? I have kids.... (sigh).

All of my friends are married or dating good men, except my close knit group. Are there any left for me, for us? I keep attracting the wrong type of men. Players, swingers, military men, preachers, and married men......why am I a magnet for foolishness? My friends, Lisa, Nicole, and Sharon are no better. My closest friends are single, too! I met each of them at different phases in life, but we all seem to have the same struggle. How does a saved woman in a relationship with Christ get through this struggle? We all attend different churches but we're all trying to live the same basic principles. God, you said if I delight myself in you that you would give me the desires of my heart. You said it and we are doing that with no fulfillment. Lord, don't say it! You don't care anything about my flesh! You are worried about my spirit. Lord, you know me. You know every hair on my head and everything I would do before it happens. Yet you continue to let me suffer with loneliness. As a matter of fact..... all of us suffer with loneliness on different levels.

Why do you allow some people to marry straight out of high school? They marry their childhood sweethearts and stay married until they die. Others you allow to meet and they live happily ever after. Then you have the audacity to allow us to get prophecies that we are getting married and we wait and wait and wait!!! Why tell us? Let us stay in the dark until he shows up. So shall it be! Woe is me..... Single, dating, and trying to remain saved!

# CHAPTER ONE

*(April praying)*

*Dear Lord, I come to you humbly as your daughter… not only thanking you for what you have done but most of all thanking you for who you are. I know my life would be so empty without you. I love you and thank you for your unmerited favor that continues to reside in my life. Lord, I thank you for keeping my family and me today. I thank you that our family circle has not been broken. Thank you for keeping us in our sound mind and keeping our physical bodies healthy. God, you are a good God and there is none like you. Lord, you promised in your word that if I delight myself in you that you would give me the desires of my heart. You know my greatest desire is to be married.*
*Lord, Pleassssssssssssssseeeeeeeeeee hear my heart as I beg and plead. I thank you again for hearing my heart. In Jesus' name I do pray.*
*Amen*

Ringgggggggggg! Ringggggggggggggggggg! Ringgggggggggg!

"Hello!"

"April, it's time to get up!" Its 5:30 in the morning already!

O my goodness. It seems like I just fell asleep. *Let me get just 15 more minutes of sleep.* I roll over and see the clock now says 6:45am. Oh my God!

Michael, wake up! Michael, wake up! We overslept! Another day of rushing. I am always rushing. If I had a husband, I could stay home in bed. Shucks, if I had a boyfriend, I could at least have a smile on my face this morning! Ugggggggghhhhhhhhhh! Rush, rush, rush! Michael, wake up and get in that bathroom.

In the car at 7:45am! Damn, I am good. Now let's get you dropped off at the bus stop so, I can get to work. Let me take my glam shot for the day! Yes that one looks good. Let's see who will receive this picture this morning. A, nah! B....Eric.....yes.....send! C, nah! D....David.....yes but let me add a good morning sexy to his. Humph! David is a banker with a Fortune 500 company. He has potential. E.....Edward...why do I keep his number? All he wants is tail! A past that I need to keep in the past. Last but not least, I can't forget Mark. Older man, tall, handsome, mature.....maybe that's what I need. Lord Jesus......I am sitting here texting! I am going to be late for work. Thank God for working close to home.

Sighing .....

Another day at Mason General Hospital. Lord, I am not for the bull from the residents, patients, nor doctors. Being a manager is what I love the most, but the politics suck. Yes, nobody is here ...yet. Great! I can check Facebook, Twitter, and my email without disturbance. Phone rings (All I do is win win, win, no matter what) Oops, I have a text! Let me cut this ringer off. Where is my churchy ring at? Let me change this ringtone. Yes, this is it!

"No weapon formed against me shall prosper. It won't work"! Yes Fred Hammond is the truth! Better yet I better put this phone on vibrate. Anyway, who

is gracing me with a text! Ahhhh.......Its David! "Good morning beautiful"! Buzzzzzzz......another text. Its Edward....what does he want? "Good
morning sexy. You know I miss you". Looking down at my phone.... *No you
don't! Your dick is hard! Your wifey, Geneva, must not be giving you none!
Let me text David back.*

"How are you handsome?" Let me text Edward back. "Hi"! He is not on my
top ten list at all. He always had ulterior motives.

Edward is a man from my past that I dated over 10 years ago. He should
have forgotten me by now. What in the devil is wrong with him? I have got
to pull away from him.  Let me get to work. What's on my calendar today?
Couple of meetings, ohhhhhhhhh yes and a lunch date with Mark.

*Lord, help me!*
***

Savannah and her loud mouth walks into the office yelling, "Gooood
Merning office mates! Howz everybody this merning?"

April responds, "Savannah, do you have to be that loud early in the morning?"

Savannah loudly responds, "Yes, girl, it's the day that the Lord has made,
let's rejoice and be glad in it!!! Be glad!!"  What's popping in here this
morning? Is your boss here yet? Has she ridden in on her broom yet?"

April responds, "Savannah, she was here when I got in. She was probably

snooping early. Her light was on in her office when I walked by so I figured she was here. Is Tyrone coming in today? He is usually here before me."
Savannah asks, "April, how was your weekend? What did you end up doing this weekend?"

April replied, "I took my son to the beach on Saturday then a birthday party on Sunday."

"I know you were in church, Ms. Churchy with your mean self!" responds Savannah.

April abruptly interrupts Savannah saying, "Smarty, of course I went to church. For your information, I went to church Saturday night for a concert then Sunday morning and evening service. On Saturday, I took Michael to ride go-carts. Friday night, I was in the Laundromat washing and drying clothes."

Savannah looks at April with the "I got gossip look" and says, "April, let me tell you what happened Friday after you left. I went to a meeting and Tyrone must've thought I was gone. I came back and the office door was locked. I fumbled for my key cause, girl, you know I never have it ready. I walked in and Shawn, one of the new residents was in the office with him with the door locked. Yes, girl, that's correct! The male resident that looks kind of fruity. They both were looking suspect when I walked in the office. Then his fruity behind said, "Well, let me head back to the unit. Call me Tyrone!" I looked at him and he was looking real stupid. I turned my head and began singing in my Erkah Badu voice, "You better call Tyrone!"
April, laughing hysterically responds, "Savannah, you are so crazy. So, you

think they got a thing going on, but Tyrone is married! Girl, Tyrone is married! His poor wife! He also has two beautiful daughters. So is he DL or Bi? You know he calls that little secretary downstairs his "work wife"! What the???? Damn! And he belongs to that big church on Fayette Street. I pass that church all the time. My sister and I say we are going to stop in and see what it's like. Damn!! That is freaking ridiculous. That makes me sick! I got to call my sister, Sharon, on this one.

*Savannah is still singing "You better call Tyrone" laughing hysterically in the background.*

April quickly dials Sharon's work number.

Ringggggggggg!!!!

April, talking to herself, says, "She better be at her desk. This is just too juicy to hold!"

Sharon answers the phone.

April interrupts Sharon's greeting with:

"Sharon, hey girl! I was about to put out an all call bulletin! I got juice!!! Guess what? This fool in here is living on the DL, Bi, or something like that. It was bad enough that he messes around on his wife. Now it is confirmed he is messing with men, too. What the hell? What is this world coming to? No wonder we can't find a man. Their asses are living wrong! And guess what, he belongs to that church we pass all the time on Fayette Street. The one we said we were going to visit. I know I am not going in there now. Don't you know someone that goes there? Then again, she church hops so much that she probably isn't there now."

Sharon responds, "April, that's crazy! Wow! I know what church you are talking about. That is the one around the corner from my mom's house. That's a big church too. What is his Pastor's name?"

April, laughing, responds, "There you go! Always asking who someone's Pastor is! Heck if I know. And girl, as wiggly as that behind is, he must be a bottomer! I will never forget that book I read that tells you how to distinguish the bottomers and toppers. Too funny! But isn't that a mess. Men these days are sad. What the devil are we going to do?"

Sharon responds, "Well I don't know about you April, but I am waiting on God. If he doesn't send me a man, I won't have one. I remember a time when I was younger when a rash of women in the church were dying from AIDS because of gay men. Now, men are marrying women and still messing with men denying they are gay. May God just take their tails on out of here before they contaminate women innocently. Since the death of my only love, you know I am picky! I will take my drug dealers any day. At least they have a good heart."

April, disgustedly responds, "Sharon, your mind is bad. They have a good heart, bad thinking, and questionable morals. Girl, you better stop playing. They aren't the best either. The hell with that! I am not settling for any of that, including a drug dealer. That mess is crazy."

Savannah yells from across the room, "April, get off that phone. We have to figure out lunch for today."

April tells Sharon, "Let me call you back. Rude tail Savannah is worried about lunch at 10am! I will call you back."

Sharon says, "Ok."

"Savannah, what do you want? You always need so much damn attention," April said.

Savannah excitedly responds, "April, let me tell you about the rest of my weekend. Let me tell you about that fool I live with. Why did he walk in my house at 1am Friday night? He claimed he was at work. He smelled like a cigar-alcohol- rotten cock factory. I was so angry. He was grabbing me claiming he was sorry. He came in with roses that I threw at the wall. I told his stank tail to go take a shower and get away from me. I fell asleep and was awakened to him eating the hell out of my stuff. It was so good that I forgave him. I don't know why I allow him back every Friday. He does it every Friday night. I don't want to be by myself. I am 30 years old. My time is running out. Who else will I get?"

April, sternly, says, "Savannah, are you stupid or just plain dumb? Then again, are you writing your own death certificate? What the hell is wrong with you? All he has to do is give you head and you forgive him? You said he came home smelling like rotten cock and you let him lay in your bed? That's the dumbest damn reason I have ever heard. You are degrading yourself to keep a man. What the devil is wrong with you? Do I need to get my oil? It's in the car. 30??? I am freaking 40 and you are crying over 30. Girl, shut the hell up before I smack you. You do not have to settle for bull. You are beautiful. You are an educated, pretty young lady with one child. Stop letting one fool disturb your atmosphere. Not to mention, you have an impressionable son. You don't want him to treat women like that. Put his raggedy ass out and do better!"

Savannah and April say in unison, "Good Morning Tyrone!"

Tyrone responds, "Good morning ladies! How was your weekend, ladies? I had a great weekend. I spent Friday evening with the fellas. Saturday, the wife and I went to a wedding. One of my boys got married. Sunday, church grind! My pastor is the best. April, you know he is doing a live recording?
 April responds, "No, Tyrone, I didn't know. When is the recording? I might have to check that out. I rode past your church Sunday. The doors were wide open. It looked like it was jumping. My sister and I always say we are going in there but haven't made it yet."

April looks at Savannah and says, "We will talk at lunch time."

"Ok," responds Savannah … "with your mean ass self."

April responds, "I am not mean. I am real and straight-forward."

April looks at Tyrone and says, "Tyrone, lets bow our head and pray for Savannah! She needs it."

Savannah abruptly responds, "Keep your prayers. I will be fine."

Savannah looks at Tyrone vĕry deviously and says, "Tyrone, did you see Shawn this weekend? You better call Tyrone!"

Tyrone sternly responds, "Savannah, NO! He was with his family this weekend."

Savannah responds laughing hysterically and still humming, "Well, Tyrone, how did you know that?" Tyrone says, "He told me that Friday."

Savannah looks at Tyrone with one eye closed and says, "O, he told you when you two were in here with the door locked?"

April interrupts and says, "Tyrone, don't listen to her! I know you are married and don't want a man, RIGHT?"

Tyrone explicitly responds, "That's right April, God made Adam and Eve not Adam and Steve! Tell her I am a married man. I love women. Ask Sharice, my work wife, how I get down!!!! I bet she can tell you about these 12 inches. Yeah, ask Sharice how I work those hips! Haha!"

Savannah sarcastically responds, "12 inches Tyrone? Please!"

Tyrone says, "Savannah, you just wish that cheating man of yours had what I have."

Savannah, now obviously upset, says, "Tyrone, mind your damn business. My man takes care of this. REGULARLY!!!"

Peacemaker April jumps in and says, "Alright, you two! Time out! Retreat to your corners before I get the damn oil!"

Tyrone responds, "Only for you because I respect you, but that Savannah is a damn witch."

Savannah jumps up and says, "Who are you calling a witch?"

Peacemaker April interrupts the bickering and says, "Savannah let it go! We have work to do. You two have been at it for the past couple hours. Cut it! Now on to more important things. Let me put my earphones in and ignore you two. I have work to do!"

April's phone vibrates.

Buzzzzz!
*Text from Edward. "Hey, what color panties are you wearing? Can I see them?"*
*How will that happen? -Return text to Edward*
*You can meet me after work. -Edward text*
*Where is your wife? -Return text to Edward*
*She won't be here! -Edward text*
*Why can't I ever tell him no? April, you have to do better. He is married. It is like he knows when I get horny. What the hell? Be strong April! Tell him no.*
*No, Edward, not today. -Return text to Edward*
*Why not? You know I love you! -Edward text*
*Call me later and we will see! -Return text to Edward*
*Ok sexy! -Edward text*

April asks Tyrone and Savannah, "Has time slowed down today? I am hungry. What are we doing for lunch crew? Savannah? Tyrone? Don't everybody answer at once. I know Tyrone brought his lunch."

In agreement, Tyrone responds, "That's right."

April looks at Savannah and says, "Ok, Savannah, it's you and me. Let's go out. Then, we can continue our conversation."

"Ok Momma April," responds Savannah.

# CHAPTER TWO

Savannah says, "Lunch was great. Thanks April. You made a lot of sense."

April says, "No problem, girlie! Anytime! Now get rid of his country ass!"

"April, you are so crazy!' says Savannah while giggling.

April says, "It is almost time to get off. *Thank God.* It's been a long day. Michael has baseball practice today. His father is supposed to take him, but I am not counting on that."

Tyrone looks at April and says, "April, is his name Robert? A guy came here while you two were gone and said he was your husband."

April angrily responds, "O he did, huh? His ass is good and crazy. I swear he is. He is my ex-husband. He is my ex- abusive husband. Did I tell you two about his mess? Well, he and I married for all the wrong reasons. One month into our marriage, he punched me in my face and gave me a black eye. To make a long story short, he pulled a gun on me the day I left. He cocked that 9mm back and it was the grace and mercy of God that I am here today. That bastard was crazy. He beat me so much that I have forgotten a lot of it. I nearly lost my mind from all his abuse. He beat and sexually abused me. I have scars to prove it. The worst part is I got pregnant. I love Michael but I wish he wasn't his father. The father of my older two, Franklin, is a much better man. He loves them unconditionally and participates in their life like a father should. He is a God-fearing man that has always raised them on God's principles. He and I didn't gel, but he is a good father unlike that trash I married. Maybe I messed up the good man I was supposed to have? I often think about how I messed up with Franklin. Tyrone, do you think it's too late for me. Do you think God will give me a husband? Singleness is so hard and frustrating."

Tyrone says, "April, I would've never guessed that you would be in an abusive relationship. You are so strong willed!"

April responds, "Tyrone, you know what? That experience made me stronger. I don't take any shit now! I will bust him in his head now and he knows it. He won't try me anymore. He knows I need medication. Saved and all... and I will beat him senseless! His abuse made me even stronger. If I shared the details of everything that happened, you wouldn't believe me. That man is straight psycho. He is re-married and beating her too. Savannah, that's why I am so hard on you. I don't want you or any woman I know to experience the things I went through. Settling has terrible consequences." Savannah says, "I got you April."

*Knock, knock, knock!*

In walks a short, thuggish looking guy who says, "Hey baby, I came by to surprise you with flowers and to take you to dinner."

Smiling from ear to ear, Savannah responds, " Joshua, you shouldn't have. Let me introduce you to my co-workers. April, this is my boyfriend, Joshua.

Joshua, this is April."

Looking him up and down, April responds, "Hmmm. Nice to meet you Josh-ua."

Savannah goes on to introduce him to Tyrone saying, "Tyrone, this is my boyfriend, Joshua. Joshua, this is Tyrone."

Looking him up and down yet staring like he has seen a ghost, Tyrone says, "Nice to meet you, Joseph. I mean Joshua."

Joshua looks at Savannah and says, "Let's step out to the empty office next door, Savannah! Again, nice meeting you all!"

Joshua angrily says, "Savannah, who the hell is Joshua? I should smack your ass against that wall. You have me coming up to your job and you embarrass me. Who is that nigga? I will handle your ass when you get home."

Savannah, obviously afraid, says, 'Joshua, it was a mistake. There is no one else. I love you and you only."

Joshua responds, "Yes, we will see when you get home. When you get there, be ready to do whatever I tell you to do sexually until I say you can stop. I am not playing with you. Be camera and video ready. Do you understand me?"

Sobbing, Savannah says, "Yes, Joshua, I understand."

Joshua demands, "Now kiss it now before I leave."

"Here?" says Savannah, "Somebody might walk in!"

Joshua says, "I don't care!"

Tears falling, Savannah says, "Ok, unzip your pants."

"And hurry up," demands Joshua. "I got to get back to work. Don't you ever embarrass me like this again! Do you understand me?"

"Yes, Joshua," responds Savannah.

Joshua says, "Now give me a kiss and get back to work. I will see you when I get home. I better have a good dinner ready cause you ruined the option of a dinner date."

"Ok Joshua," says Savannah.

April looks at Tyrone and says, "Tyrone, it's awfully quiet over there. What do you think is going on?  Let's listen at the wall. Tyrone, do you hear anything?"

Tyrone says, "No, April, I don't hear anything."

"Me neither!" says April

Savannah re-enters the office.

"Bye Joshua! I love you!" says Savannah.

April and Tyrone, both, drop to the floor like they are searching for a lost item.

April says, "Tyrone, did you find my earring I dropped over here. You got young eyes."

Tyrone responds, "I don't see it April."

April responds, "I found it Tyrone. O, hey Savannah. You know I am about to punch you in your face right?"

Savannah responds, "April, why?"

April says, "You let that little runt of a man show off on you? I know you stupid now! You can pop him on the top of his head. Better yet, do you want me to pop him for you?"

Savannah says, "No, no, April. I got this. I will be fine. It is time for me to punch out and get out of here anyway. I have to stop at the store and pick up something for dinner."

April says, "Savannah, I thought he was taking you out to dinner."

Defensively, Savannah responds, "No, he got a text from work. Plans changed. I didn't feel like going out anyway. Ok...I'm out! See you guys later."

Savannah looks at Tyrone saying, "Well, Tyrone, she left here pretty abruptly. What do you think of that?"

Tyrone says, "April, I believe he is abusing her. Did you notice that heavy makeup she had on Friday? That MAC was packed on that face! She is covering up something."

April says, "Tyrone, if he is beating her, it will come out. I am going to keep talking about my abuse and see if she breaks under the pressure. I am going to keep praying for her too. You need to do the same thing. She needs it. I am going to bring some oil in here too. I am going to snuff that demon out. She is having a birthday dinner next week. I am sure he will be there. I got something for that tail."

Laughing, Tyrone says, "April, I love you! You are so churchy! Snuff that demon out, huh? You are too funny!"

April says, "Tyrone, there is nothing funny. She is in a serious situation. We have to do something to help her. I was an abused woman. I know what happens eventually. I am pissed now. I am so sick of women settling for no good men just to avoid being single. Savannah belongs to that Methodist church in Pasadena. I think it's called Mason Memorial AME church. I wonder what the heck they are teaching her cause she is worth more than that. He probably does that same manipulative stuff my ex-husband did. Maybe I can take her to the gun range when the girls and me go next week. If she sees the power behind firing a gun, she may consider putting some lead in his ass!"

Tyrone says, "April, you are crazy! That won't work. Her self esteem needs to be built up first."

April agrees and says, "You are right. I need to pray about this tonight because I need to do something before I consider doing a drive by! I can't stand to hear about one of my saved sisters getting abused. She is worth so much more than that."

**Knock knock knock!**

Shawn, the resident, says, "Hey Ty!" Tyrone, looking crazy, says, "What's up Shawn?" April looking and laughing says, "Ty? Yeah, it's like that! On that note, I am out. See you two tomorrow. "You better call Tyrone!"

Buzz Buzz... April's phone is vibrating in her purse... who is texting me now when my hands are full? They have to wait until I get to the car. My hands are too full to reach in my purse for that phone.

Buzz Buzz .... Wait wait, I am coming!

Now I have two text messages.

*April, I will be late so can you take Michael to the field and I will be there. – Robert Text*

*Do I have a choice? – return text to Robert*

*Ok – Robert text*

*Now who else is texting me? It's Edward.*

*What's up sexy? – Edward text*

*Hi – return text to Edward*

*What time can I see the color of them panties? – Edward text*

*I will let you know because I have to take Michael to the field. – return text to Edward*

*Ok, I am waiting sexy! – Edward text*

Why do I fool with his ass? Love is a terrible emotion.... or is it lust?

Buzz Buzz ... Buzz Buzz.....
*Hey beautiful – Eric text*
*Hey handsome – return text to Eric*

Buzz Buzz ....
*Hey pretty lady – Mark text*
*Hey sir – return text to Mark*
*So what do you have planned this evening? I will be up in that area. I am staying at an area hotel for a conference. I will be up around 8. Can I see you? – Eric text*
*Would you like to accompany me to dinner, lovely lady? – Mark text*

Decisions, decisions? Who should I go out with? Ugh! Decisions! Eric is a good screw. Mark is the gentleman that I haven't even kissed yet. He is so kind and sweet. Do I want romance or sex tonight? Better yet, why am I settling for any of it when I want a husband!!!! This can't be the way to get a man. I am turning into a player. JESUS, help me! The word says he that findeth, not she that findeth. Only God would have wisdom to know we are too freaking fickle and emotional to make those types of calls. She that findeth.....That's a funny thought!

*Eric, what time are you talking? – return text to Eric*
*Mark, what time do you want to see me? – return text to Mark*
*Around 6 – Mark text*
*9pm – Eric text*

(April thinking) O yeah! I may be able to do both. *April, what are you doing?* You are supposed to be an example to other women and you out dating multiple men. Shit, I am not sleeping with all of them. God knew I would be in this place and he knew I would be making these types of decisions. Men do this all the time. What they don't know won't hurt them? I am single, saved and bored as hell. I am tired of sharing my bed with pillows.

*Ok Mark, where? – text to Mark*
*Eric, where are you staying and I can't stay late – text to Eric*
*Outback on York Road – Mark text*
*Sheraton in Towson – Eric text*
*Ok see you soon – text to Mark*
*Ok see you later. Send me the room number – text to Eric*

Yeah yeah! Let me get this boy to practice. His father better not be real late or it's him and me. I got 2 dates. It's right at my cycle too. Every woman knows that is the hardest time to resist a man. I am going to get some tonight! Hahahaha!

April arrives at the restaurant. She greets Mark.
Mark says, "Hey pretty lady! I know you like pink roses. Here you are!"

April responds, "Aww Mark, that is so sweet! You are a sweetheart. I have to give you a hug!"

(April thinking) Alright April, he deserves a kiss for this.

Mark says, "You are a pretty little young thing with some luscious lips. Thanks for the hug and kiss." (April thinking) This is why I like older men. They don't require much. Just give their old tail a pat and kiss and they are good.

April says, "Thank you for inviting me to dinner, Mark."

"Anytime beautiful!" says Mark.

April says, "Now, Mark, I have to leave by 9pm. I have to pick Michael up from practice."

Mark responds, "No problem, baby! Anytime I get to spend with you is good! So, April, when are you going to invite me to your place? I would invite you to mine but I live so far away."

"Well, Mark maybe next week," says April.

Mark says, "Cool baby! Let's order some dinner. April, are you ready to order?"

"Yes sir I am!" says April. Well thank you for dinner love!"
Mark says, "No April, thank you! The pleasure was all mine."

Buzz Buzz .... Buzz Buzz ....
April says, *"Excuse me Mark, let me check this."*

*Room 678 – text from Eric*
*Ok, I am on my way – return text to Eric*

April and Mark walk out of the restaurant,

April says, "Thank you Mark. Text me and let me know you made it home safely."

"I will indeed sweetheart," says Mark.

(April thinking) Now off to get this monkey off my back and put this fool to sleep.

April arrives at the hotel and knocks on the door.

*Knock knock knock …*

Eric says, "Hey pretty lady! I am glad to see you. HE is glad to see you."

"I see he is since he is saluting me," April giggles.

Eric responds, "Hahahaha! You seem to have that effect on me. Come on in. Let me take that blazer. Damn you are sexy!"

April's phone begins to vibrate.
Buzz buzz …. Buzz buzz … Buzz buzz …
April says, *"Excuse me let me check this phone!"*

Baby, I am waiting! – text from Edward
Delete text!
Eric asks, "Is everything alright baby?"

"Yes, Eric, everything is good," responds April.

Eric says, "I have been thinking about you all day".

April asks, "Eric, will this ever go beyond a casual moment? I enjoy spending time with you in/out the bedroom. We both have relationships with God. We both have thriving careers. Do you ever want to get married? You know my desire is to get married."

Eric says, "April, shhhh, lets enjoy the moment. We will talk about that tomorrow. Let me see you. You are so sexy. Don't destroy the moment. I promise we will talk tomorrow after my meeting. Now let's get more comfortable."

. . . . . . .

# CHAPTER THREE

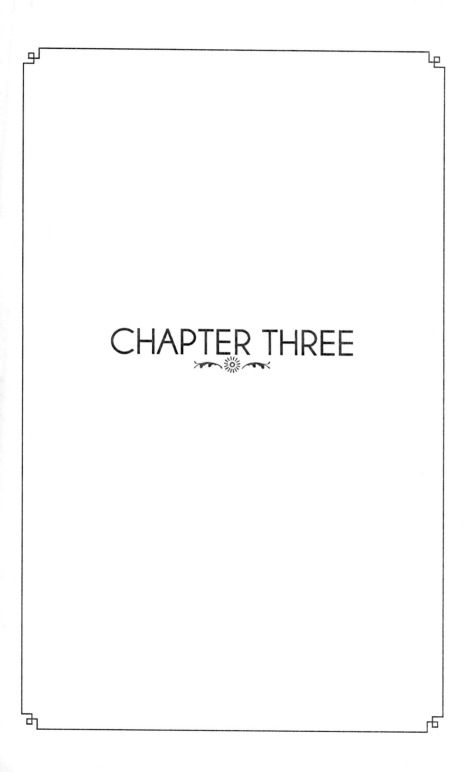

> *(Sharon praying)*
>
> *Dear God, I come to you as humbly as I know how. As a servant, I reference and respect your holy and righteous name. There is no greater love than the love you give to your children and for that alone, I love you with my whole heart. God, thank you for your undying love, grace and mercy that you continually give your children. God, cover my family, friends, and anyone within the sound of my voice. God, you know my desires. You made me. You know I delight myself in you not for things but because of who you are. I know that all things work together for the good so I patiently wait on your manifestation of my good thing. I love you. In Jesus Name, I pray, Amen*

Sharon and I have been friends since college. We met during our sophomore year when she transferred in from Spelman College. She was a very pretty, dark skinned, tall, shapely girl. We were in the same English class. We were placed in the same group and the rest is history. Sharon comes from a large family where she is the oldest of 6. Sharon's father is the Pastor of a mega church, Jackson Street Freewill Baptist Church, in Atlanta. I used to visit her family during breaks and we would hang out for a few days.

Time has made us family more than friends. She is my big sister.

Now don't get me wrong, Sharon's family was not perfect. I remember one summer I was there and we overheard her parents arguing about his infidelity. Sharon and I had just come in from the club when we heard all of this loud noise. They were fussing so loudly that they never heard us come in.

We went into Sharon's room and could hear Sharon's mom say, "What the hell is wrong with you? You didn't think you should use a condom and not just protect you but also protect us! Now you have an outside child! What will the people say? I lend you to them Sundays, church meetings, revivals, and anything else church related. Yet, my payback is I can't trust you."

Sharon's dad, Rev. Morris, said, "Lend me? You didn't and don't have a choice. You knew what my life entailed when I met you. You knew I was preacher. You knew I traveled around the world. Besides do you think I am stupid? I know Marvin, our first child isn't mine. I found the paternity tests you had performed. I kept quiet then. . . and now you want to crucify me! Go to hell! You would've never known I found those papers. You are just sloppy! What would the church think about that, Mrs. First Lady?"

The argument continued on for a few hours until we heard doors slam and lots of crying. Sharon was very upset and apologetic about the argument.

The next morning, everyone was at the breakfast table eating and smiling like nothing ever happened. I never understood it, but it was never discussed again. Sharon and I became family from that moment forth.

Untold situations like this that were never discussed became the catalyst for the troubles that would plague Sharon. The summer of 1994, Sharon met a handsome young guy, Troy, at Club Choices. Troy was light skinned, had curly hair, and stood 6 ft 3 inches tall. He was the average pretty boy. He was obviously a drug dealer. His attire, flashy jewelry and the countless bankrolls made it evident that he was a "pharmaceutical salesman". Troy was not the average corner thug. He was high on the echelon. He was a kingpin. He had a fabulous home in Owings Mills. All of his neighbors were either ball players or local businessman. No one in his neighborhood knew his business. He was good at hiding what he really did.

One look at Sharon and he was in love. Sharon fell for him instantly. They talked on the phone all the time. He was taking her to the finest restaurants and buying her the latest designer styles. It wasn't like Sharon wasn't used to designer names, but this time it was different. Sharon was in love. I was very afraid for her. Sharon was very naïve. Coming from a rich, upscale neighborhood, Sharon was very disconnected from the hood. I tried to help her but before I knew it, she was under the spell! She was holding packages for him. She was delivering packages for him. Sharon officially became a drug dealer girl. I will never forget the look on her face when she came to tell me she was pregnant. It was our senior year in college and she was crying uncontrollably. I thought he hit her or broke up with her the way she was crying.

With tears in her eyes, Sharon says, "April, I don't know what to do."

April responds, "Do? Sharon, what's wrong?"

Sharon, crying harder, says "I am pregnant April. He is ecstatic. This is his first baby, but I am scared. I am not ready to be a mother yet. He wants to get married, but I am scared. What will my dad say? What will the church think? What should I do?"

April responds, "Sharon, calm down. Let's think about this. You are 21, last year of college, and pregnant. We can get through this. Do you want to marry him?"

Sharon responds, "April, I don't want to marry a man just because I am pregnant. Troy has promised me on several occasions that he would get out of that world but it's like he can't. I am frustrated. I don't want to raise a baby in that type of lifestyle. My mom and dad don't even know his real lifestyle. They think he is a student with us."

April asks, "Sharon, how far along are you?"

Sharon says, "I am 3 months pregnant."

April asks, "Sharon, have you considered an abortion? I know you come from a religious home but it could be an option."

Sharon says, "April, I can't kill a baby. Besides, how will I pay for it? Troy wants the baby. He is happy. I will just have to tell my parents but I will finish college."

April responds, "Ok, Sharon, I am here for you regardless of what you decide. Remember, we are sisters for life."

As fate would have it, Sharon decided to keep the baby. Little Tarsha wasn't here yet but we were all tickled watching Sharon's belly grow.

On June 15, 2 weeks, after graduation, Sharon's mom hosted the biggest baby shower for her new granddaughter! It was fabulous. It was held at the Marriott Waterfront in the grand ballroom. Over 500 people were in attendance. The ballroom was elegantly decorated in beautiful hues of pink and lavender. It was a seated affair that would have made anybody jealous. Sharon was absolutely glowing in a custom made Vera Wang maternity cocktail dress. Troy was in matching Polo style. They looked so cute. Just as we began to take pictures of Sharon and him in the baby shower hat, he surprised everyone. Troy asked if he could say something.

Troy says, "Sharon, I have loved you from the moment I saw you across the room in the club. You have evolved from my friend to my girlfriend and now to the mother of my child. I love you and now I want us to be a family. Sharon, will you marry me?"

There was not a dry eye in the room. He presented Sharon with a beautiful princess cut 2-carat solitaire. It was gorgeous.

Sharon said, "Troy, I love you and YES!!!"

It was a Kodak moment. Everyone was so happy. When the event was over, we had to rent a U haul truck to get all her gifts home. It was a wonderful evening. What was a baby shower became an engagement party. It was a beautiful night.

As we were pulling up to Troy's house, we noticed a light on in the foyer. Troy never leaves lights on. He is so energy conscious or should I say cheap! Anyway, Troy asked everyone to stay in the car while he, his brother, and two friends checked the house. The two friends went around back while Troy and his brother entered the front door. As they entered the front door, we heard, Pop, pop, pop! I screamed and we both ducked down. Sharon immediately started crying. As I looked up, I saw two men, dressed in dark clothing, run across the lawn. The two friends ran from around back and started firing guns at the two but they missed. They ran back to the house where Troy was lying face down in a pool of blood unresponsive. His brother was shot in the back but he was still breathing. All I could yell is "Call 911, Call 911!" but it was too late. By the time, the police and ambulances arrived; Troy and his brother were dead.

The happiest day turned into the saddest day in a matter of hours. We buried Troy and his brother 1 week after the shooting. The shooters were arrested 2 days before the funeral. The shooters were his own street level salesman who had come to burglarize his home. Startled by the door opening, they shot Troy as a reflex. They both confessed to the shootings. At his death, Sharon was 7 months pregnant. Sharon wouldn't talk, eat or drink for weeks. We were all talking to her but she wouldn't answer. It was becoming really bad. I tried telling her that she had to eat for the baby's sake. The mention of the baby made her cry. April says, "Sharon, you have to drink! You have to eat! You can't starve the baby!"

Sharon yells, "How can I eat or drink? The love of my life is gone. I don't want to raise Tarsha alone."

Just as Sharon said those words, she began to keel over in pain. She fell to the floor and went unconscious. Screaming, I called 911.

April begins to pray: *Lord, this is April. I don't know how to say fancy prayers with big words so here goes. Save my sister! Don't let anything happen to her, Lord. I need her. I love her. Lord, please PLEASE heal her!!!*

The paramedics arrived and took her to University of MD Hospital. I called her parents who also promptly came to the hospital. We were all asked to wait in the waiting room. Finally, the doctor approached us. Hi, are you the family of Sharon Morris?

Synchronized, we answered, "Yes. Is she alright?"

I am Dr. Yates. I am the doctor attending to Sharon. She is doing well. She is very dehydrated and we are giving her fluids. Sadly, the baby died. The baby's cord was around his neck and the lack of fluids caused the cord to tighten and ultimately choke the baby. We delivered the baby 15 minutes ago. Sharon is still very disoriented and groggy. Would you like to see her and the baby? Please, no more than 3 visitors at one time.

Cries were heard all through the waiting room as we listened to the doctor. Finally, her parents and I went in first.

As we entered the room, my eyes immediately looked over at the baby swaddled in a blanket with a hat on her little head. She weighed 7 pounds 3 ounces and she looked just like Troy. She had chubby cheeks, light skinned and coal black curly hair. She looked like she was just sleeping. I looked over at Sharon and she was sleeping like a baby. Then the strangest thing occurred. I looked over and saw Troy sitting in the rocking chair holding Tarsha. I blinked. I rubbed my eyes. My eyes began to water because I just knew I was now losing my mind. I kept staring and he was smiling holding Tarsha in his arms. As I walked closer, he disappeared.

Mrs. Morris kissed Sharon on the cheek whispering quietly, "Hey baby, its mommy and daddy. We are here."

Sharon awakened slowly saying, "Hey mommy, have you all seen Tarsha? I haven't seen her yet. I haven't heard her cry. Where is she? Who does she look like?"

Mrs. Morris quietly replied, "Sharon, Tarsha didn't make it, baby. She died. The umbilical cord strangled her and they couldn't save her. It was too late."

Sharon looked over at the bassinet and saw Baby Tarsha lying lifeless swaddled in a blanket. The screams that proceeded would have raised the dead. Sharon hollered and screamed so loudly that the doctor and nurse ran into the room. Seeing Sharon so hurt caused everyone in the room to break down and cry. Sharon asked to see and hold the baby. The nurse wheeled the bassinet over to the bed and handed the baby to Sharon. Sharon hugged Tarsha and cried uncontrollably. None of us could do anything but stand near her bedside. Sharon peeled back the blanket to see her little hands and feet.

Sharon screamed, "God, why? I am sorry. I didn't mean it. I want my baby. I need my baby. What did I do to deserve this? First Troy, now Tarsha. No!

Bring her back. Lord, I want my baby!"

Rev. Morris immediately began to pray. *"Let's pray! Heavenly father, we come to you as humbly as we know how. Heavenly father who sits high and looks low, you know our circumstances and God we know you are in control. Heavenly father, send your healing angels to watch over my baby girl and our new guardian angel, Baby Tarsha. Heal Sharon's heart."*

Sharon burst in on the prayer. All her tears dried up and she loudly proclaimed, "I hate God. He took Troy and now Tarsha! I hate him."

Rev. Morris continued to pray. *"God, we need you now in this room. Send your grace and mercy. We know you don't make mistakes and we may not always understand your will, but God we trust you!"*

Sharon yelled out again. "No we don't. You took my fiancée and now my baby. I HATE GOD!"

Mrs. Morris tried to comfort Sharon but she was at a point of no return. Sharon looked at me and said, "April, why? What did I do to deserve this? April, help me!" April replied, "Sharon, I don't know. I can't answer any of your questions."

That moment in our friendship changed Sharon's life forever.

# CHAPTER FOUR

Ringgggg. Ringggg.

April says, "What's up girl?"

Sharon responds, "Hey April. What's going on?"

April says, "Nothing much Sharon. I was just thinking about our college days. We had so much fun. Can you believe Tara was 3 when we met and she will be graduating college this year? We have been through some things."

Sharon, affirmatively, responds, "Yes April, we have and you are still crazy as ever. One day I am going to call Dr. Richey and tell her you need a pill just like your kids."

April says, "Girl, shut up. I don't need a pill".

Laughing, Sharon says, "Yes you do April. . . just like Granny!"

Laughing April responds, "If I need one Sharon, you and I both will be on the same medication!"

Sharon begins reflecting and says, "Tara is 21 and Tarsha would have been 18. Wow! I remember the day I couldn't say her name without crying. And I would have been an old married woman by now. Well, at least God gave me a chance to feel real love. I don't ever want to get married now. Single is good for me."

April responds, "Sharon, you can have that. I have washed, wiped, and cleaned too many little ding dings between Michael and Ryan. It's time for God to give me a big, long ding ding to play with. I want a husband. This single thing is for the birds. I don't see how you do it, Sharon. I love the touch and smell of a man! You are just chilling. . . . . . You and God, huh?"

Sharon says, "April, I don't need all that. I am content with the friends I have. They may be doing a little hustling on the side but they have good hearts. I deal with them when I want to and on an "as needed" basis."

April says, "Sharon, will that "good heart" get them into heaven? How do you still deal with drug dealers after what happened to Troy? That incident didn't scare you straight?"

Sharon says, "April, they have good hearts. We all sin and fall short. No sin is greater than another. Sex, lying tongue, gossip, and crimes are all weighted the same. Just because they sell drugs des not make them bad people. They have good hearts. They treat me with respect. I don't go as far as I used to with Troy. I don't hold packages and I don't deliver anything. They know I am a "church girl" and they respect that."

April says, "Sharon, are you losing your mind? Does the devil have your mind? Do I need to cast a demon off you? The oil is in the car. Good hearts? When does a good heart get a person into heaven? When does a good heart make a person saved? You are a saved, holy ghost filled, speaking in tongues Christian. They are lustful, dope slinging, drug abusing good-hearted men, right? Your tail has lost your mind. Do you ever talk to them about your parents and your upbringing? Do they know about Troy? What the hell is going on?" Sharon says, "April, calm down!

First off, how did we get on this conversation? I do not and will not be discussing this issue with you. This is between God and me. He is the only one that can judge me and that's the end of story. I love you like a sister but stay in your lane."

April says, "Love me like a sister? O yeah? Well, I don't want to bury my sister because she has chosen to sleep with the enemy. Why can't you date a Christian? Why can't you date a man that isn't a drug dealer? You must have a demon. You have to have a demon. I am talking to the demon, not Sharon because Sharon can't be this crazy. The Sharon I know and love wouldn't say such a stupid thing out of her mouth. The Sharon I know wouldn't question which lane I am in. Just know I am in a tractor trailer on that bumper about to make you crash into your car "IN YOUR LANE" if you don't stop talking crazy!"

Sharon says, "April, we will talk later. I need to get back to work. I am supposed to meet Lisa today for lunch. She is coming here for an appointment. Talk to you later."

# CHAPTER FIVE

Lisa is the "holy roller" of the group. She wears the long dresses, no makeup, and no jewelry. She is high yellow, wide hips and small waist. She is a very pretty girl. She has always been a mystery with all her secrets, but her lifestyle leaves many peepholes into who she really is. She has a blossoming career as a high school principal where she has worked over 20 years. She has her Master's Degree in Education and is pursuing a PhD in Education. She is very intelligent and highly motivated about her career moves. Lisa intends to be the Superintendent of Howard County Public Schools. With her looks, personable character, and intelligence, she is a shoe in!

> *(Lisa praying)*
>
> *Dear Lord,*
>
> *Awesome, mighty, wondrous God whom I love with all my heart. I come to you first asking for your divine forgiveness for every sin I have committed. I know you know my heart, but I can't control myself. Every time I say I am going to stop, abstain, and wait on you.... I end up falling again. God, you said you would not take this desire away from me because it is a God-given gift but help me! I can't control myself. I am begging. I want a husband, but I keep having sex when the urge hits. I need help! God, I thank you for your sovereignty and your mercy.*
>
> *In Jesus' Name I pray..... Amen*

(Lisa singing) In the name of Jesus, In the name of Jesus, we have the victory! O, in the name of Jesus, Satan you have to flee. O o o, tell me... who can... stand be-fore us... when we... call on that great name!

Ringgggg! Ringggg! Lisa answers phone.

Praise the Lord!

(deep voice of Lester) Hey Baby!

Lisa replies (choking), "O, hey Lester!"

Lester says, "I enjoyed you last night, Lisa!"

Lisa replies, "Yes, I told you I live by John Legend's song! (singing) Best you ever had, I hit you with the back stroke!"

They both giggle!

Lester replies, "So can I get some more of that tonight?"

Lisa says, "Well, I have church tonight! You can come over when I get home."

Lester replies, "That sounds good."

Phone beeps. Another call is coming in.

Hold on Lester. Let me answer the other line.

"Hey girl," says Sharon.

"Heyyyyy," says Lisa.

"Why do you sound so happy this morning?" says Sharon.

"Aww, nothing! Just in a good mood. Oops, hold on!" says Lisa.
Lisa clicks over.

"O, I am so sorry baby. That's one of my girlfriends. I will see you tonight," says Lisa.

Lester replies, "Ok, baby. Can you wear my favorite color tonight?"

Lisa replies, "I sure can. See you later. Bye."

Lisa clicks back over to Sharon.

"Hello, I am back," says Lisa.

"You are mightily giggly! What's going on?" says Sharon.

"We will talk this afternoon. I am coming into town for an appointment. We are still on for lunch, right?" says Lisa.

"Yes," says Sharon.

Lisa says, "See you later, girl."

Ringggg. Ringggg.

April says, "Sharon, I forgot to tell you something earlier. I had a dream about Lisa last night. You know I never dream about people I know. The dream was weird. Lisa was walking with a dark shadow along a dark road, half clothed. She looked dazed. We were watching her from the side, calling her name, but she couldn't respond. There was a bright light ahead of her, but it kept getting farther away because the dark shadow was holding her. It was strange, but scary. I know your girl is so super-holy but I think trouble is lurking."

Sharon responds, "That's funny because I just hung up with her. We are meeting for lunch today. She was so giggly this morning. Something is up with her sneaky ass. She wears those long skirts and no makeup."

April says, "I told you that Lisa is probably getting more ding-a-ling than all of us! All that "praise the Lord" is a cover up for "Don't stop, get it get it!" (in her Luke voice). It will come out!"

Sharon, laughing, says, "Girl, you are so crazy! Well I will let you know after lunch today! I will call you later. Bye"

"See ya girl," says April.

Ringggg! Ringggg!

Sharon Morris, how can I help you?

Lisa says, "Hey Lady! I am downstairs. Are you ready for lunch?"

Sharon responds, "Cool, I am on my way downstairs."

As Lisa and Sharon are walking to lunch, they run into Lester.

Lester looks startled to see Lisa.

"Hey babe," says Lisa.

"Oh, hey Lisa," says Lester very nervously.

"Lester, this is Sharon. Sharon, this is my honey, Lester," says Lisa.

They respond simultaneously, "Nice to meet you."

Concurrently, a very petite, pretty young lady approaches and says to Lester, "I am ready, honey."

"Honey?" says Lisa.

Lester nervously says, "Lisa, this is my fiancée, Monique. Monique, this is Lisa."

Monique says, "Nice to meet you Lisa."

Lisa looks startled and hurt at the same time as she says, "Nice to meet you."

Monique responds, "Very nice to meet you. Look at my ring. He just proposed this morning when he picked me up from the airport. I just love this man."

Monique looks at Lester and says, "Well, honey, we have to get going so we can meet my mom and dad at the restaurant uptown."

Lester looks at Lisa and says, "See you later?"

Almost in tears, Lisa says, "Have a great lunch."

Sharon notices the tears in Lisa eyes.

Sharon asks, "Lisa, what's going on? Who is he?"

Lisa starts to cry, but responds, "The man I was so happy about this morning that I was going to tell you about over lunch. I thought he was the one. He just left **MY** house this morning."

"Aww Lisa," responds Sharon, "I am so sorry!"

"I just don't understand. I have a great relationship with God, attend church regularly, pay my tithes, and offerings, pray frequently, have a successful career, own my home, own a nice car, no kids, but I can't seem to find a trustworthy, honest man. I really thought he was the one. He has been at my house every night this week. But now I see why.... She was out of town. Then, he proposes right after he leaves my house. Why?" says Lisa. Lisa's phone rings......

"Freak me baby, just like that. Let me lick you up and down til you say stop"...... Lisa's ring tone for Lester

"No, he is not texting me," says Lisa.

"What is up with that ringtone? Let me find out you a freak!" as Sharon bursts out laughing.

Lisa reads the text while rolling her eyes at Sharon.

*I love you Lisa and we need to talk – Text from Lester*
*Love me? Do you think I am stupid? – Lisa's response to Lester's text*
*Come on girl. You know I like that good-good you got! And I will be over tonight so we can talk. – Text from Lester*
*What do we have to talk about? You made your choice.- Lisa's response to Lester*
*Church girls are the biggest freaks and I am going to get that even if it is one last time. So I will see you tonight – Text from Lester*
*See you tonight – Lisa's response to Lester*

Sharon asks, "What did he say?"

Lisa responds, " Nothing girl. I don't want to talk about him anymore. New subject."

Sharon responds, "Aww hell naw! You won't get off that easy. I know your freaky ass. You are going to listen to his bull just like you did in previous relationships. When will you recognize your self worth? You don't have to keep giving these men your ass to hold him. Has this one taken you out in public or does he just show up at midnight for a booty call? You are beautiful, successful, and you have so much to offer the right man, not a right now man. What the hell is wrong with you?"

Lisa, sadly, says, "I am 45 years old and there isn't a prospect of a man. I meet men all the time in business meetings, when I am out of town, and in the office. They always **compliment** me and my style. They ask me out for drinks and maybe dinner, but we always end up in bed. I like sex. I love sex. What's wrong with that?"

Sharon responds, "You are a freak! A jump off! A skeezer! A hoe! A whore! A dumb ass! Too damn easy! You have a demon! Who the hell told you to give up your ass to every Fred, Joe, and Perry that buys a $5 drink and $30 dinner? Is that all you are worth? You are worth diamonds and rubies, but your dumb ass is on sale for a 99-cent Snicker bar. There is nothing wrong with dating when you don't sell yourself out so easily. Sex! Sex! Sex! Do you have any self-control? You sit in church every Sunday with those long ass dresses on, no makeup, and no jewelry! You get out of church and turn into a concubine, prostitute, and street crawler. This is a mess and I bet you will let that dummy back in too."

Looking dumb, Lisa responds, "Ok Sharon, did I have to be all that?"

Sharon looks at Lisa straight in her eyes and says, "YES! It's ironic that this all happened today because April had a dream about you last night. All I am going to say is don't let the darkness consume you so much that you no longer see the light! In your words, new subject!"

Lisa, still obviously upset, "Ok Sharon I understand. Tell April I said thanks." Sharon responds, "You have made me so angry that I am not hungry. We are having a wings and wine ladies night on Friday. I expect you to be there."

Lisa responds, "I will be there. I promise. I need to sit down with the girls for a good crying and laughing session. People think it's hard being a woman, but it's even harder to be a saved, single woman. Every move you make is watched. Each year you aren't married, you are questioned. Being single and saved is another ball game. I don't see how you hold it together. I look at you and think "how can you maintain without a man?" I can't do it. I am not you Sharon! I need companionship. I want companionship!"

Sharon responds, "I don't expect you to be like me, but I want you to feel whole. Are you happy with yourself? Why do you keep choosing men that use you for your body? Why do you give **EVERY** man your tail? Why do you let them talk to you like you are a 2 bit ho? Friend, I just want you to stop being a freak. You are almost 2 people in one. A shouting, speaking in tongues . . . I am afraid to say holy ghost filled . . . . Because your keeper is not keeping you . . . . . . . Lady! At night, you turn into somebody I don't recognize or know. Listen to your damn ring tone. Suppose that goes off in church one day, then what? One minute, you are hollering. . . praise the Lord and the next minute you are trying to get sexual healing! What the??" Lisa says, "I understand and I heard everything you said. I will continue to work on me."

"Great. Now I have to get back to work," says Sharon.

"Thank you for listening, Sharon," says Lisa.

"That's what friends are for," says Sharon.

They embrace and part ways.

Walking back to her office, Sharon begins thinking to herself.

"Ok, God. I can help everybody but myself. I just talked to Lisa about her situation but I can't stop dating these drug dealers. I lost my fiancée and my child to that lifestyle, but I haven't learned my lesson. I know you said gifts and callings are without repentance and I know you called me. If anyone finds out about the type of men I date, it could ruin my integrity. God help me. Move those type of men out of my life."

Thinking so hard, Sharon bumps right into a guy. She looks up and he is a short, stout, young, refined gentleman that is casually dressed. Sharon recognizes him because he is a Pastor at a local church. He looks at Sharon in her eyes. Sharon begins apologizing profusely for bumping into him. As Sharon is apologizing, she hears the voice of God say, "Can you believe me for him?" Sharon is thoroughly convinced that she has a concussion until she hears the voice of God again say, "Can you believe me for him?" The man says to Sharon, "Its ok. I am ok. Are you ok?"
Sharon responds, "Yes, I am."

The man says, "My name is William. You look familiar. I pastor the church in Randallstown named Johnson Square Church of God in Christ. Wait, I know who you are. You are Morris' daughter. Morris from Atlanta. Am I correct?" Sharon responds, "Yes that is my father. My name is Sharon Morris. Very nice to meet you, William. Again, I am so sorry that I bumped into you. I was so busy thinking that I was not paying attention. Please accept my apology." William responds, "I accept your apology. It really was no big deal especially when a pretty lady bumps into you."

Sharon begins thinking again. "Lord, you are crazy now because I don't do fat men and I surely don't do preachers or pastors! Lord, stop playing. Am I being punked?"

William says, "Do you work in this area? I am down here often meeting clients."

Sharon responds, "Yes, I work in that building across the street."

William asks, "I hope I am not being too forward, but could I take you to lunch one afternoon?"

Sharon smiles and responds, "Sure."

They exchange phone numbers and depart in separate directions. While walking away, William turns back and looks at Sharon's little waist and big hips like she is a big chocolate doughnut thinking. . . . "Well thank you Jesus!"

Sharon looks back and sees a short, fat man thinking... "O Lord, O Lord, why hast thou forsaken me!"

Sharon walks in her office and grabs messages from her secretary. Sharon sits down at her desk and reaches for the phone. Just as she is about to answer the phone, her office phone rings.......

Sharon Morris, How can I help you?

"Girl, where have you been? I have been calling you. How was lunch?" asks April.

Sharon responds, " I had the most eventful lunch I have had in years. Lisa has mad drama and I literally bumped into Pastor Michaels. I was day-dreaming and nearly knocked him down."

April says, "Pastor Michaels? The fat, short one?"

Sharon responds, "Yes and he asked me out to lunch."

April is now laughing hysterically, "What did you say? No, Hell no, which one?"

Sharon slowly says, "We exchanged phone numbers and I said yes."

April is now laughing even harder. "You said yes to a FAT man. The chick that only dates drug dealers. The chick that says she will never date a minister, preacher or pastor! The chick that only dates tall, skinny men. The chick that says a FAT MAN better close his eyes and not look at you. The chick that says she doesn't climb any mountains! You lying!" says April.

"I can't stand you. Do you know how much I can't stand you? I couldn't tell him no because he knows my father. I couldn't be rude. One lunch date won't hurt," says Sharon.

Rolling on the floor laughing like she heard a good Kevin Hart joke, April says, "One lunch date huh? God just set your ass up! You thought you would continue to date good hearted, drug dealers! Your time is ticking, First Lady!"

"Shut up! Did you set me up? How you know God set me up? They do have good hearts. First Lady? Never! I never want to be like my mother and never see my husband. Besides, I don't want a husband. I just want a baby!" says Sharon.

Ringggg......Ringgggg! Sharon's other line rings.

Sharon says, "Hold on April."

"Sharon Morris, how can I help you?" says Sharon.

"Hello Sharon, this is William. William Michaels. I know this is short notice and we just met, but I have an event to attend Saturday night and I need an escort. Are you available?" says William.
Sharon says, " Can I check my calendar and get back to you this evening?"

William responds, "Yes you can. I have mid week service tonight at 730pm, but I should be home by 10pm. You can call after 10pm if that's not too late."

Sharon responds, "No, that isn't too late because I have service myself tonight. Talk to you later tonight."

William responds, "Great. Talk to you later."

Sharon returns to the call with April.

"I am back, " says Sharon.

"You know I am loving this, right! God made you bump into a fat man and now you are forced to go out on a date with him. I love it. I bet you won't say what you won't do no more, Missy!" says April.

"On that note, I have to get back to work. I will talk to you later. Bye April." says Sharon.

April begins to sing, while laughing , "The overweight lover in the house, the overweight lover in the house!"

Sharon begins to think, "What am I going to do? I don't like FAT men. I can't hurt his feelings. Lord, you made me and you know my preferences. Lord, I don't even want a husband. Why are you doing this to me? A **FAT** man!!! Lord, o Lord, why hast thou forsaken me? I can't bring disdain to my dad's name by being ignorant. I must utilize tact in this situation. He was very cordial. He isn't ugly. He can lose weight. Sharon, why are you thinking ahead of yourself? He might not like you."

"Will you believe him for me?" says God's voice.

"Sharon, girl, you must be losing your mind now. You must have been in that sun too long today. God wouldn't do this to me. Believe God for a **FAT** man! Do I have to go out with him. People will automatically think we are a couple. You know how the saints do – always freaking assuming! They will look and say is that pretty girl with that **FAT** man! Perception is a beast. Then not only is he **FAT**, but he is short, too! What happens when I wear my heels? I will look like a giant over him!"...... thinks Sharon.

"Will you believe him for me?" says God's voice.

"We are not ashamed of the gospel of Jesus Christ"....... Sharon's ring-tone on her phone

"Hello," says Sharon.

"Thanks for your words today, girl," says Lisa.

"You are welcome," says Sharon.

"See you Friday night," says Lisa.

"Ok," says Sharon.

# CHAPTER SIX

> *(Nicole praying)*
> *Dear God,*
> *Most humble and faithful Father who sits high and looks low. Most of all, I thank you for your faithfulness toward me whenever I feel far from faithful to you. You look after me when I fail to look after myself. I thank you for every small and large blessing that you continue to bestow upon me. Thank you. Lord, please forgive me for every sin I commit knowingly and unknowingly. Continue to place your hedge of protection around me when I don't deserve it.*
> *In Jesus' name I pray,*
> *Nicole*

"You know I love you, don't you?" says Anthony.

"Yes, I do," replies Nicole.

"Why are you always praying to that "God" of yours? If he hasn't answered you yet, why don't you consider Allah?" says Anthony.

"Allah? Haven't we had this discussion before? I am strong in my faith. Religion is not a subject we are going to discuss. I love Jesus Christ," says Nicole.

"That isn't the name you were calling last night when I was ....... (laughing hysterically)," replies Anthony.

"Well, I did call him a couple times when you ahhhh........ no, we won't be discussing that right now. Besides, I need to get dressed for work. Are you going job-hunting today? You have been out of work for a year now," whispered April.

"I will drop you off at work and I will see how I feel," says Anthony.

"Why do you need my car if you aren't job hunting?" replies April. Laughing, Anthony responds, "I need to take my girl out to lunch and pick little Anthony up from school!"

"You aren't funny. You really aren't. You better not have anyone in my car," says Nicole.

"Girl, I was just playing. You can't take a joke. I love you. You are my queen," says Anthony.

"Get up, I am ready! Come on so I can get to work on time. I get off at 4. Don't be late today like you were yesterday," says Nicole.

"Got you!" says Anthony.

"I want you to go to church with me next Sunday. This is not a good example for my kids with you laying up in here and not working, especially for my son," says Nicole.

"Didn't I tell you my mother is a Pastor and I have no desire to go to a church building? You all are brainwashed! Allah is the truth; not Jesus. Jesus was just a Prophet. One day, you will listen to what I say. I see a lot in churches that I don't like. You dummies giving all your money to that woman or man that calls themselves a Pastor. That mess is sickening. Half of the music ministry is sleeping with each other or sleeping with plenty of other women. The Pastor is hitting his wife and smacking half the women in the congregation. The director of the choir is more feminine than you. Most churches are Sodom and Gomorrah, including my mother's church. Anything to keep members and keep the money coming in. Pastor driving a Benz and his members are standing at the bus stop. The truth will set you free. Haven't you heard of Farrakhan? You want me to transform into a **man of God**, but you have never heard the true and honorable Farrakhan. Church is a gimmick and I am not falling for that bull," says Anthony.

Nicole responds, "You never told me your mother was a Pastor. So now I get it, you were church wounded. Farrakhan, huh? Really? Every church is not like that. I am not going to argue church and its principles. Just like the Muslim religion has its traditions and principles, so does Christianity. Considering you grew up in the faith, I am sure you are aware. Brainwashed? Sounds like you are wearing that hat yourself. My trust is not in man. My trust is in God. I have a relationship with God, not man. Where you are.....I was there some time ago. Church hurt is the worst. When you have faith and believe in a thing, you don't judge man's actions. God will handle him. Every man or woman of God that is living foul will meet his or her fate. Nobody is perfect but some things should not happen. Integrity is everything.

That is why I am getting convicted about this foolishness we are doing. You and I have been seeing each other for over 2 years and no mention of marriage."

"Diarrhea of the mouth is what they call that disease you have. Always running your mouth. I told you I am not ready for marriage. And I am not marrying a lady that isn't Muslim. We have a good time and I do love you. I want you to convert. Aren't you going to be late? Lets go!" says Anthony. As they drive to work, Nicole notices a "roach" on the floor of her car.

"Are you smoking in my car?" asks Nicole.

"What are you talking about?" asks Anthony.

Nicole responds, "I was not always saved. I know what a roach looks like. I should punch you in the face."

Anthony responds," Girl, chill. It relaxes me. I wasn't driving. It must've fell out of my pocket."

"Allah says it is ok to smoke huh?" asks Nicole.

# CHAPTER SEVEN

*Nicole arrives at work. All of her co-workers are looking strange.*

Nicole jokingly asks, "What's wrong? Did somebody die?"

Nicole's boss, Director of Operations of Hanson & Associates, Mr. Randolph, responds, "Yes, Nicole have a seat. I have some bad news. Dr. Hanson and his wife were killed over the weekend in a skiing accident."

"My Dr. Hanson? You are lying," says Nicole.

"Unfortunately, Nicole, it's true. The family is in the process of making arrangements. Julie, his daughter, is trying to arrange everything but she is so young," says Mr. Randolph.

"I can't believe this. I just saw him Friday. I told him to have a good trip and see him Monday. I had no idea he would be gone on Monday," cries Nicole.

You could hear quiet sobs all around the room.

"Who will I administratively take care of now? I have been his personal assistant for the past 15 years. He and his family were like my family. Oh my God!" screams Nicole as she begins to break down.

Mr. Randolph says, "Nicole, that is why I didn't call you at home. I got the call at 3am and I haven't slept since. God is a keeper and as a woman of God, I know you understand. God will see his family and us through this. I will give you a minute but this business must go on and we must do some work today."

Nicole responds, "This a sad day at Hanson & Associates. But you are right; we will get through this. I will call Julie to see if I can help her. I can call my family friend, Mr. Edward Williams, owner of Williams Funeral Home because he is reasonable and does good work."

"That sounds like a good idea. I know she may need a level-headed person to help her since most of their family is out of town," says Mr. Randolph.

"Thank you Mr. Randolph. Let me call Edward and give him a heads up," says Nicole.

*Ringgggg! Ringgggg! Ringgggg!*

"Good morning, Williams Funeral Home, how may we help you?" says a pleasant older woman.

"Good morning, can I speak with Edward Williams?" says Nicole.

"He is presently working with a family. Can I take your name and number and have him call you back?" says the receptionist.

"Yes, my name is Nicole and my number is 443-555-2345. Thank you," says Nicole.

The receptionist responds, "I will make sure he gets your message. Have a blessed day."

***

"Nicole, hey girl, how are you?" says Tammy, one of Nicole's co-workers.

"I will be okay. It was such a big shocker. I would have never guessed I would have walked into this news this morning," says Nicole.

Tammy says, "I know this isn't a good time, but I need to share something with you. I debated telling you, but I believe it's best because too many sisters live in secret."

"Yes?" responds Nicole.

"I was at my sister's house Friday night and I saw your car parked at the corner store. Her and I sat out on the front porch. My sister saw him getting in the car and told me to check that handsome dude out getting in that car. She continues to tell me that the dude lets other dudes poke him in the butt. I asked her how did she know and she said everybody knows. He gets high and that's how he pays for his habit. She further explains how the young drug dealer will poke anything with a hole and that's why HIV is so rampant among that young group. I didn't tell her that I knew him. At one point, she said his name. I was blown away," says Tammy.

Nicole, with tears in her eyes, says, "Huh? What? You are lying!"

"Nicole, I am sorry. You do not have to believe me. Just watch his behavior. Do some research. So many of our sisters die of AIDS from men who don't care about anyone but themselves," says Tammy.

Nicole says, "I can't talk anymore. Just leave me alone for a while!"

*Ringggg. Ringggg. Ringgg.* Nicole's cell phone begins to ring.

"Hi Nicole. This is Edward. How can I help you today?" says Edward.

"Hi Mr. Williams, one of our physicians died over the weekend and I wanted to recommend you for their services," says Nicole.

Edward replies, "Oh yes, give her my personal cell phone number. It is 410-555-0179. Tell the family I will come to their home to set up arrangements." "I will pass this information on," says Nicole.

"How is the family? I haven't heard from you all in a long time. How is April? Tell her I asked about her," said Edward.

Nicole responds, "Everyone is doing well, thank God. I will let April know you asked about her. Have a good day!"

"Talk to you soon," says Edward.

Buzzz . . . . . . Buzzz. . . . . .

"Now, who is this? I can't handle any more news today!" says Nicole.

*Hey girl – text from April*
*Girl, girl, girl – text from Nicole*
*What's going on? – text from April*
*What ISN'T going on is a better question? Call me – text from Nicole*
*Calling now – text from April*
*"You make me happy! You make me whole! You take the pain away. I'm so in love with you" – (Nicole's ringtone)*

"Hello. Hold on one second, ok?" says Nicole.

"Hey girl! What's up?" says April.

"I need to step outside for a minute. Mr. Randolph, I will be back shortly," says Nicole.

"Ok, take as much time as you need," responds Mr. Randolph.

Nicole says, "Girl, today is one the roughest days of my life. I come in the office and find out Dr. Hanson and his wife died over the weekend."

"Girl, I am so sorry to hear that. I know you really loved him and his family. What happened?" says April.

"I really don't know yet. I am waiting for his daughter to call me. I just got off the phone with Edward," says Nicole.

"Edward who? I know you don't mean Edward Williams. I know that bastard didn't ask about me!" says April.

"Hahaha! Thanks for that laugh. Yes, Edward Williams, the man you should have married. Your boo. Your baby," says Nicole.

Nicole starts singing ... "That's just my baby daddy. That's just my baby daddy."

"Winch, you are not funny! That man hurt me to the core. I loved him. He was my first true love. Then he turned around and married the beast that is bamboozling him with that tomato soup and spaghetti. When are men going to recognize that witchcraft is real and a woman can do their asses in!" says April.

"Yes I am funny. Hahaha! Men don't believe girl. They think they are invincible. All it takes is ONE! I guess his one got him. But you must have whipped something on him because he has not forgotten you. Let me find out you got tricks," said Nicole.

"Every woman has a trick, tramp. But if you don't get in his head first, the tricks don't work. You are just a notch in his belt buckle. Anthony must be doing some tricks on your ass since you won't let his trifling behind go," said April.

Crying, Nicole says, "Girl I am hurting so bad! I just don't know what to do." "Nicole, you will be ok. The shock of the death has you right now but God will mend your heart," says April.

"No, no, something else has happened. It's Anthony," cries Nicole.

"Did that mutha put his hands on you? I can do a drive-by," screams April.

"No, no, he hasn't put his hands on me," says Nicole.

"Ok, then what happened cause he could come up missing," says April.

"Awww, April, I don't know. This morning, he drove me to work and I found a roach in my car," says Nicole.

"Nicole, you are getting me crazy cause you found a bug in your car? Are you stupid or something? I am about to call the crew and you are crying over a freaking roach? Clean that dirty ass car!" screams Nicole.

"No, April. Roach as in weed, ganja, reefer, chronic, trees," says Nicole.

"Gotcha, but I am still missing the issue," says April.

"Ok. That is an issue because I told him no smoking in my car. The real issue is what I was told by Tammy, my co-worker. She saw him in her sister's neighborhood, over East, buying drugs and he is known as the BOTTOMER," cries Nicole.

"What? On top of being a lazy, no-good, non-working, freeloading son of a," says April.

"Don't say it! I can't believe it. I can't believe he is letting men poke him in his butt. He has shown no signs. He never tries to poke me in my behind. He doesn't act gay. As a matter of fact, he talks boldly against homosexuality.

Maybe it's me. I have gained so much weight in the last year so he isn't attracted to me anymore," says Nicole.

"I know your ass is on crack along with his stupid behind if you are blaming yourself for his unfaithfulness. First of all, we have to figure out if it's true. We need to do some surveillance in that neighborhood to see if he really shows up. Secondly, I better not ever hear you use your weight as an excuse for him to be a butt hole. Call him and tell him you have a ride home today. I am picking you up. We need to talk in person and create a plan. Meanwhile, I know a few people that live on the East Side so I will start the research. A lot has happened today, but get your mind right. We gonna catch this mutha," says April.

Nicole, still crying, responds, "Ok I will call him and let him know. Thanks April."

"Anytime, girl. This is what friends are for. I wasn't always saved and saved does not equate to being stupid so we got some work to handle. See you after work," says Nicole.

"See you later," says Nicole.

As Nicole hangs up, her phone rings. It is Julie, Dr. Hanson's daughter. "Hi Nicole," says Julie.

"Hi Julie. I am not going to ask how you are doing because I know this is hard. I called to offer my help in coordinating the funeral. A family friend owns Williams Funeral Home and he is willing to come out to your house and set up arrangements. I can come meet you and help you if you'd like," says Nicole.

"That would be great. I need all the help I can get," says Julie.

"Ok, I will let Mr. Randolph know I am leaving. I will call Edward and give him your address. I will be there shortly. One of my girlfriends will have to bring me. Is that ok?" says Nicole.

"No problem. See you soon," says Julie.

Ringggg. Ringggg. Ringggg.

"Hello Edward, the address is 13415 Grandier Road. I will be coordinating the funeral alongside the family. What time can you come? It is now 10am," says Nicole.

"Hello Nicole. That was quick. I can be at the house by noon," says Edward.

"Great. See you at noon. Bye," says Nicole.

"Bye," says Edward.

Ringggg. Ringggg. Ringggg.

"Hey girl, what's up," says April.

"Girl, I know this is last minute but can you pick me up and take me to the Hansons' house by noon," says Nicole.

"Sure, I will take you on my lunch break. I will be there by 11:30. See you in a minute," says April.

"Thanks girl. See you in a minute," says Nicole.

Nicole walks back into the office and heads to see Mr. Randolph.

"Mr. Randolph, I am leaving at 11:30. I talked to Julie. I am going to meet Mr. Williams at her house to get the arrangements together," says Nicole.

"Ok, Nicole. Let me know if I can be of any assistance. Let Julie know that my family and I are praying for her," says Mr. Randolph.

# CHAPTER EIGHT

*Nicole and April arrive at the home of the Hansons. Edward Williams is already there. They walk up to the door and ring the bell.*

Ding Dong!

"You know Pastor Holcumb lives in this neighborhood. I think that is his house across the street. It sure is. That's his car," says April.

April turns and walks to the car and notices an additional car in the driveway.

"Wait a minute! Is that Edward's car?" says April.

"Yes. Be nice," says Nicole.

"Be nice? You winch, you set me up. You didn't tell me HE would be here," says April.

Door opens and Julie answers.

"Nicole, thank you for coming. Thank you!" says Julie.

Nicole and April walk into the house. Julie leads them to the library of the house where Edward is seated.

As April enters, she catches eyes with Edward who looks at her like he has x-ray vision undressing her with every step.

April is dressed in a form fitting black wrap dress that slips very nicely over her small hips and rounded butt. Her dress drops low enough in the front to capture her well-endowed cleavage.

Edward is 6ft 2inches tall, approximately 200 pounds. He has a dark complexion and his skin is as smooth as a baby's bottom. He is dressed handsomely in a navy blue suit with a pink French cuffed dress shirt with blue cufflinks. His shirt is accented with a blue and pink bowtie. Nobody can wear a bowtie like Edward.

Edward gives April the look. You know that "I like that freak 'em dress" look. April looks at Edward in disgust.

"Hi ladies. It is good to see you again, Nicole," says Edward, as he reaches out to hug her.

"It is good to see you too, Edward," says Nicole.

Looking at April like he could undress her on the spot, Edward says, "it is always a pleasure to see YOU April."

Edward reaches out to hug April and she places her hand out to shake his hands. They shake hands and sit down.

Julie looks so sad and absent from the room.

Nicole walks over and sits next to Julie.

"I never thought I would be burying my parents before I got married or had children. My mom was supposed to help me pick out my wedding dress. My dad was supposed to bounce my son on his knees. I won't hear my kids say Pop-Pop or Grand mom. What am I going to do, Nicole?" asks Julie.

"Julie, we will never understand why God allows certain situations to happen in our lives. The only thing we can be assured of is that God doesn't make mistakes and he will help you cope," says Nicole.

"My Pastor lives across the street. Maybe I can walk over and ask him to come over and have prayer with us," says April.

"That would be nice," says Nicole.

"I will be right back," says April.

April gets up and walks to the door. Edward watches her every step like a dog in heat panting. Nicole watches him shaking her head. Nicole gets up to get Julie something to drink.

Nicole walks past Edward and says, "You are whipped. I wonder what wifey Gina would say about your behavior. Calm down and start the freaking arrangements."

Edward begins to talk to Julie about what he can offer. Nicole walks in with the water and hands it to Julie. The three of them discuss it and settle on some arrangements.

*Ding Dong!*

Nicole walks to the door. April is standing in the doorway with Pastor Holcumb.

"Good to see you again Nicole," says Pastor Holcumb.

"Good to see you as well, Pastor," says Nicole.

Pastor Holcumb walks up to Julie and embraces her.

'Julie, I didn't know your dear mother and father passed away. I would have come over sooner. Your dad said he was coming to my church this Sunday. He called me "The Radical Young Preacher." He was a good man. Your mother would always tell me that I needed a wife. She would always say I was too handsome to be all by myself," says Pastor Holcumb.

"What can I do? Would you like to have the services at my church? I apologize sir," says Pastor Holcumb.

"Hello, my name is Edward Williams, owner of Williams Funeral Home. Thomas? Man!" says Edward.

"Ed, what's up dog? I haven't seen you in ages. You own a funeral home now? Wow, man! It is good to see you," says Pastor Holcumb.

April and Nicole look at each other in disbelief.

"So, we have scheduled the funeral for Saturday morning at 10am. The viewing will be Friday from 3pm-9pm. The family didn't have a church home. Can the services be held at your church? What do you think about that, Julie," says Edward.

"I think my parents would love that," says Julie.

"Thank you for the honor, Julie," says Pastor Holcumb.

"Well, Julie, I must head back to the funeral home. I will make sure your parents are picked up and brought to the funeral home today. Can you make sure I get clothes for the two of them by tomorrow afternoon? Thomas, can you lead us in a word of prayer before we go our separate ways," says Edward.

"Sure," says Pastor Holcumb.

"I will make sure you get everything you need, Ed," snickers Nicole.
"Yeah, Ed, Nicole got you," mimics April.

Let us pray . . .

Most Holy and righteous Father, we come to you humbly asking for your unsurpassable peace for this family. You are God and God alone. We know you don't make mistakes but we ask for your merciful love, grace and peace for this family, O God. God, send your ministering angels in this place to help your daughter, Julie, cope with your will. We count every request as done and we bless your Holy name.

In Jesus' Name, we pray ... Amen

"Thank you again, Julie. If there is anything you remember or anything you need, don't hesitate to let me or Nicole know," says Edward.

"April, walk Edward to the door, please?" asks Nicole.

April gives Nicole the "Your ass is grass and I am the lawnmower" look.

Nicole smiles as they walk to the door.

"Man, take care and we will catch up soon," says Edward to Pastor Holcumb.

"Yes, man, we will, " responds Pastor Holcumb.

When April and Edward reach the front door, he asks her to step outside.

"Baby, I texted you a few days ago and you never returned my phone call," says Edward.

"I can't keep sleeping with you. You go home to lay next to Gina while I hug my pillow. It is getting old," says April.

"Girl, you know I love you. I just can't get enough of you. I see your pictures and my man instantly rises," says Edward.

"You are the one that got married. I am still single. You said you got married to preach and you still sitting on the pew. You hurt me and I can't keep hurting myself. You aren't leaving Gina," says April.

"Ok April. I love you and I always will love you," says Edward.

April walks back in the house.

As April enters the library, she sees a veil upon Nicole's head. She also sees a tuxedo on Pastor Holcumb. The two are engulfed in a lively conversation so they don't notice her staring at them. Julie has gone to the bathroom, so April doesn't immediately enter. She waits and watches. Julie returns and so does April.

"Nicole, I have to get back to work. Are you staying or do you want me to drop you off home?" says April.

"I would love if you and Pastor Holcumb would stay here with me at least until my aunt and uncle get in this afternoon," says Julie.

"Well, I don't have my car today. I rode with April," says Nicole.

"I can drop you off in town when I go later today. It's not a problem and please call me Thomas," says Pastor Holcumb to Nicole.

Nicole responds, "Thank you Thomas, but I don't want to inconvenience you!"

"Oh, it's not an inconvenience. It's my pleasure," smiles Pastor Holcumb.

"Well it has been decided. I will pick you up from your office, Nicole, when I get off this evening because we have plans, remember," says April.

Looking dazed, Nicole responds, "We do?"

"Yes, we have a detail, remember, Cinderella?" says April.

"Cinderella? We will talk later. Okay, see you later. Let me walk you to the door," says Nicole.

"Ok Pastor, see you soon and thank you. Julie, you are in my prayers," says April.

April and Nicole step outside.

"Why did you call me Cinderella? He is so nice. He is a real person. I can't believe the great conversation we had," says Nicole.

"Because God is taking you from the fields to the palace, friend! I saw you. I also saw something else, but I can't tell you yet. Anyway, girl, see you later. Enjoy him," says April.

April pulls off and Nicole goes back in the house.

Buzz Buzz Buzz . . . .

"Who is texting me," says April.

*I still want you – text from Edward*

*I want you too but not to share – April text to Edward*

*Just give me time – text from Edward*

*Time? I had you first. You married Gina while we were together and you want time. Good joke – April text to Edward*

*I mean it. I should have married you – text from Edward*

*Why do you do this to me? You know I have a weakness for you - April text to Edward*

*Cause you love me too – text from Edward*

*I do but this has to stop. I am driving. TTYL - April text to Edward*

*Ok. I will call you later because I want to see you today – text from Edward.*

# CHAPTER NINE

*"Praise Him, praise him. Jesus blessed Savior you're worthy to be praised. From the rising of the sun until the going down of the same. He's worthy. Jesus is worthy. He's worthy to be praised,"* sang the choir at God's Church of Praise.

"I love to hear the choir at your church," says Nicole.

"We are guaranteed to get a good word up in here. Pastor Holcumb is always on time with that word," says Lisa.

"Sing choir," yells April.

Buzz Buzz Buzz . . . . . . . . .

"Who the heck is texting me in church?" says Lisa.

*Hi baby – text from Lester*
*You know I am in church – text from Lisa*
*YOLO and I miss you – text from Lester*
*I will call you later – text from Lisa*
*Promise? – text from Lester*
*Yes – text from Lisa*

"That better had been Jesus texting you," says April.

"He makes me feel the glory sometimes," says Lisa.

"You nasty heifer. We are in church," says April.

"We will talk after church over dinner," says Lisa.

"Praise the Lord Church! My name is Tiara Jones and I have your morning announcements. Today is Sunday, May 15 and this is your week's announcements. This evening at 7pm, we will be worshipping with All Saints Baptist Church on 5535 Martin Luther King Boulevard where Pastor Jason Vann is the Pastor. Pastor is asking the Youth for Christ Choir to sing and the Warriors for Christ Step Team to perform. This is their Youth and Young Adult Day so we are asking all youth, young adults and young at heart to support Pastor. On Monday, we will have prayer here in the sanctuary at 730pm. The women will be in charge. Administrative Pastor, Simone Simms will be the pastor in charge. Midweek service will be held on Wednesday night at 7pm. Wednesday night is a dress down service. This has been your morning announcements. Have a blessed week," said Tiara Jones.

A man, approximately, 5 feet 6 inches, about 180 pounds in excellent shape about 40 years old approaches the podium. He has a caramel complexion and he is handsomely dressed in a 3 piece tailored black pin stripped suit with a red pin stripped shirt accented with a paisley tie and black polished dress shoes. It is none other than Pastor Holcumb.

"Your Pastor is so handsome. And he is single too. Mmmmmm," says Lisa.

Pastor Holcumb begins to speak.

"You may be seated. Well church it has been an interesting week. Over the last week, I have performed 1 wedding for one of our own and 2 funerals. One of our dearest church mothers, Mother Shirley Johnson passed away at the ripe age of 100. I also performed a funeral for one of my neighbors, The Hansons, husband and wife. You never know the day and hour that God will call you home. He told me he was going to visit my church this weekend. I didn't think it would be this way. I also performed a wedding on Friday night for one of my young ministers. Mr. and Mrs. Shaun and Ana Saunders, please stand up," says Pastor.

The church applauds.

"This couple is a beautiful couple that had their wedding here Friday evening. The Saunders' are an example of young love that has blossomed into a mature love. These two are high school sweethearts, but they didn't rush God's process. They waited until God said it was time. Ana didn't pressure Shaun and Shaun waited until he heard the voice of God say it was time. They, both, are now college graduates with budding careers and a deep love for God and each other. Their relationship is a living example of what I teach about. Today, I am very proud of the man Shaun has become. He is a true man of God and it made my heart proud to make them one yesterday. Ana is an example of a virtuous woman and the young ladies of the church could learn a lot from her," says Pastor.

He tells the couple to be seated. The audience applauds.
Let us pray.

*"Dear Heavenly Father, Ruler of Heaven and Earth. I thank you for your twins, grace and mercy that followed us into this place today. Lord, I thank you for your people. Lord, I humbly thank you for choosing me as a vessel to be used by you any way you see fit. Lord, I ask that you move in this house like never before. Lord I ask that I decrease and you increase in this place. I dispatch an angel to every seat in this church. Let every angel remove the scales off of the eyes and ears of your children. May they not hear me but I want them to hear only you. You are the true and risen God and I thank you!*

*In Jesus' name, I pray..... Amen*

"Now give God some praise for what he has already done!"

"I can't hear you!"

"Wait a minute. if that praise was for me, I would say ok, but it's for the one that woke you, kept your family circle complete, blessed you in spite of. Now lets try this again.....GIVE GOD SOME PRAISE!"

*The church erupts in praise.*

"Take your seats if you can. The word that God has given me today is a hard one but a necessary one. That's why I dispatched angels first because so many of you will get sleepy or ignore me."

"I talked about Shaun and Ana first because what God does for one, he can do for everyone. Young women, wait on God. The devil knows what you like and he will always send a counterfeit before he sends the real one to keep you distracted. I know you all want a handsome looking man like me but.....

Church laughs.

Lisa says, "Amen, I sure do. I'll take you."

April looks at Lisa in disgust and says, "You have a demon!"

Pastor continues his sermon.

"Sometimes we want what we aren't ready for. We pray and get specific with God about what we want physically in a man or woman but we forget all the internal buttons they need. Yes, buttons! Some of you, women, are crazy. We need the ability to deal with you when your hormones tell you to act like a monster. You know you all get crazy for nothing."

"Men, we can be handfuls too. In my previous marriage, I married what looked good. She had a fabulous body and she was gorgeous. I didn't need her to talk. She was my trophy. Needless to say, that was the beginning of my troubles. I didn't care what kind of mind she had nor did I care about her goals and ambitions. As long as she looked beautiful everyday and stood beside me as my prize, I was good. Over time, that wore out. She became pregnant with our only child together, Pamela, and that saying is true: if you have a girl, she will take all of your looks when you are pregnant. Well, my ex started to look like a monster. Pamela was born and she is my baby girl that I love with all my heart. This was in the beginning stages of ministry and God was beginning to reveal my gifts. As a young Prophet with no intentions of becoming a Pastor, I began to see my ex from the inside out. Inside she was full of spirits that couldn't go with me to the next level. By the time Pamela was three, we were headed to divorce court after only five years of marriage."

"This brings me to my topic for today. Stand up. Look at your neighbor, pointing at yourself, and say "This one right here!"

"Turn with me to I Samuel 16. Let's stand for the reading of the word. Lets start at verse 6 and read together."

> 6 When they arrived, Samuel saw Eliab and thought, "Surely the Lord's anointed stands here before the Lord." 7 But the Lord said to Samuel, "Do not consider his appearance or his height, for I have rejected him. The Lord does not look at the things people look at. People look at the outward appearance, but the Lord looks at the heart." 8 Then Jesse called Abinadab and had him pass in front of Samuel. But Samuel said, "The Lord has not chosen this one either." 9 Jesse then had Shammah pass by, but Samuel said, "Nor has the Lord chosen this one." 10 Jesse had seven of his sons pass before Samuel, but Samuel said to him, "The Lord has not chosen these." 11 So he asked Jesse, "Are these all the sons you have?" "There is still the youngest," Jesse answered. "He is tending the sheep." Samuel said, "Send for him; we will not sit down until he arrives." 12 So he sent for him and had him brought in. He was glowing with health and had a fine appearance and handsome features. Then the Lord said, "Rise and anoint him; this is the one." 13 So Samuel took the horn of oil and anointed him in the presence of his brothers, and from that day on the Spirit of the Lord came powerfully upon David. Samuel then went to Ramah.

"You can now be seated," says Pastor.

"Complaining is a daily habit like brushing your teeth. God, where is my husband? God, I am lonely. God, I want a wife. God, I don't have any money. God, why did he hurt me? God, why did she cheat on me? God, why are you making me wait? Complaint after complaint after complaint. Have you ever noticed that children don't complain? They may not have real responsibilities but they never complain. Complaining starts when we become adults. David was the youngest of eight and he was the one who went through the most. He was left outside all day taking care of sheep. He was a child but he took care of the sheep happily. If I left you out front of the church on a hot day for 30 minutes, I would hear more complaints than Carter got liver pills."

Church laughs and people shake their heads in agreement.

"Sometimes before you open your mouth to complain, you need to think over your life and see every obstacle that God allowed to come your way and how you overcame it. It's amazing that we think before we thank. We pout before we pray and we punch before we praise. Change begins with you. Change your mind. Change your attitude. Change everything."

**"AMEN,"** yells Sharon.

"David had the hardest life of all his brothers but God still favored him. Look at somebody across the church and point at yourself saying, "This one right here!" When you choose to see yourself the way God sees you, you will see a change. Favor is not fair. Last does not mean least. If David had that thought, he would have never had the courage to throw his small stone at the giant. When you see yourself differently, you don't settle.

Saved ladies, you don't allow a drug dealer to date you. What does he have to offer you? Saved ladies, you don't allow a man in jail to dictate your life. If he went to jail, that was your parole so move on and shut up! Saved men, a lady that has no goals and ambitions other than a sugar daddy is not for you. Saved men, a lady that doesn't respect herself is not ready for you. And since I am on this subject, if a man comes to the altar today and asks God into his heart, he is not ready for you, vultures that will run after him next Sunday. Chill out! If I catch any woman in my church chasing a man like a cat chases a mouse, you will hear from me! Have some respect for yourself. Let God clean that man up first, establish a relationship with God and get himself together!"

**"Preach Pastor,"** yells April.

"Let me clear up a rumor. From the Pastors to the pews, the wife God has for me is not a part of this church. I am a single man. I don't date secretly and I am not sleeping with anyone. I am praying about her. So, all the temple whores can chill. You are not her! The "her" I want you have no idea what she looks like so don't waste your money getting any plastic surgery to enlarge your lips, butt, or breasts. Save your money. You all know I keep it real. Integrity has made this ministry grow. So you keep it 100 because I always will."

"To my saved ladies, this is my public service announcement for today. From this moment forth, do not make an appointment to talk to me about a man that you freely gave your panties to and now you are so torn up because he hasn't called you anymore. Stop being a free-cock Molly! Churchwomen down through the ages have the reputation of being freaks. Break the cycle and just say NO! My name is Thomas Holcumb and I approve this message!"

The church stands, cheers and yells, **"AMEN PASTOR, PREACH!"**

Nicole begins to looks a little uncomfortable so Sharon reaches over and asks, "Girl, are you alright?"

Nicole responds, "Yes, I am cool. Why do you ask?"

"No, you don't! Pastor has stopped on your street and parked huh? Sure, his "her" isn't a member because he wants Nikki Poo! Hahaha," laughs Sharon.

"Shut up," says Nicole.

"God has a window of blessings to give you when you make a decision to let him show you YOU! Be an original not a counterfeit. Look at my brother, Timothy, over there. He can get away with things that you all better not try. He never tries to be anybody else and that is what I have respected about him, growing up. He didn't walk a chalk line but he was respectable. He did him! Be yourself. No man wants to date his mother and no girl wants to marry her father. Be the GREAT you that God created you to be. Again, look at your neighbor and say, "This one right here!"

**"O, you are preaching Pastor,"** yells April.

"Stand up. God wants you to see yourself like he sees you. You are destined for greatness. A moment of loneliness should not write a lifetime of heartache. You deserve better. When people begin to judge you as God processes you, just point at yourself and say, This one right here! You are not ready! Now the ministers are at the altar and I want everyone who doesn't see himself or herself in greatness to come down here and get prayer. Self-esteem is a killer. Low self-esteem is a bad recipe for a saved person. Men and women, come now so we can touch and agree for a change in your mind. I pray that each of you get a visitation from God himself the next time you look in the mirror. I want you to see yourself as he sees you! Come now. Choir, sing."

Choir sings quietly, "I need you. You need me. We're all apart of God's family. Stand with me. Agree with me. We're all a part of God's family."

"Pastor Simone, come up and do the benediction," says Pastor Holcumb as he takes his seat.

"Church, lets thank God for this awesome man of God that God has given us," says Pastor Simone.

The church applauds.

"Now unto him that can keep us all from falling. Be blessed and we will see you this evening," says Pastor Simone.

# CHAPTER TEN

The ladies decide to go to dinner at Outback.

"How did you all enjoy the service," says Sharon.

"It was great," says April.

"Lisa? Nicole?" asks Sharon.

Lisa is busy texting and doesn't hear Sharon.

"Who are you texting?" asks Sharon.

"Somebody who text me," says Lisa.

"Anyway, Nicole, what about you? Pastor Holcumb is the truth and he is young, too. I love his "keeping it 100" ministry. I have seen the good, the bad and the ugly as a PK. Pastors can talk a good game from that podium, then do everything they are big and bad enough to do after church. As a minister under his leadership, I have learned to respect ministry again. These jack lags out here will make you run from church and never come again," says Sharon.

"Hahahahaha! But that dumb Simone is going to be just like Diana Ross with her hair all over her head in *Mahogany* banging her head up against some padded walls when he doesn't marry her. She thinks she got him sewn up and he doesn't pay her dumb ass any attention. It's funny to me to watch her act like she is the first lady when she is actually the last lady! I think he has a fondness for Nicole but her crazy ass wants that slimy ass Muslim, ANTHONY! Hahhahaaha," says April.

Nicole replies, "You don't know what I want. I enjoyed the service today and it made me think but, shit, I don't know what I want. Anthony is a decent man, I hope. He is just a Muslim. It may be fine. I will invite him to church. April, that man is not interested in me. What gives you that idea, anyway? Why are you laughing at Pastor Simone?"

Sharon jumps in and says, " You two chill. Listen! Pastor Simone is different. She does show off but she isn't dumb enough to try me especially since she knows my father is a Pastor and she can look at me and see I don't take any mess! April, you don't have any respect. She is Pastor Simone, not Simone. Any who, she does make it appear that something is going on between her and Pastor Holcumb. But I must say, he doesn't look at her twice. Perception is a beast. She uses perception to her benefit but it seems to be backfiring. I think Pastor Holcumb does have an interest in you, Nicole. He asks about you all the time. How is Nicole? He encourages me to invite you to his services so maybe you should get yourself together because, girl, he is watching you!"

Nicole replies, "Me? Get myself together! Who says I want to marry a Pastor? That is not a cakewalk. That isn't a glamorous life. That's a mess. I have three children. Why would he want me? Please! You both can save that. I love Anthony. I just want him to get saved and that is who I plan to marry."

April says, "Jobless, freeloading, "I just want your booty" Anthony! Are you stupid or something? And on top of that, he's a **BOTTOMER!** Nicole, you are a well-educated young lady that loves the Lord so why in the hell do you want a bum? He is a freaking bum. He doesn't work and isn't looking for work. What does he offer you but a wet behind? A toy can do that. He doesn't pay bills. A toy only requires batteries. I may not like you all the time but I have always thought you were a pretty, educated lady (no homo)! Hahaha! You deserve better. I see a first lady in you. You have the demeanor. Besides, wait and see what God says."

All the ladies say in unison, **"BOTTOMER?"**

"Yes, we did a surveillance and caught his country ass living wrong. The only thing that has saved him from getting got is Nicole. I don't know why she won't let him go. We saw him in action with our own eyes. I wanted to jump out the car and do a "Cheaters" episode on him. I had my video camera with me too. Do you all want to see it? Anthony does not deserve Nicole. His trifling ass could bring you herpes or even worse AIDS! You don't need a man like him. You deserve so much better. God wants to give you better but you have to let go of what you have. What do you have to lose?" says April.

"April, you really need medication, but I give you your props. You missed your calling. You should have been an investigator. You remember that time we caught your father. This crazy girl can catch anybody. She is good. Cheaters? Girl, you could have your own show! I can see it now!" says

Sharon.

"Please, men play too much, so when Nicole called I jumped into action. I do what I do for the upkeep of mankind. Otherwise, women would be catching charges or dying of AIDS at a faster rate. It is my civic duty especially for my sisters in Christ. Now as for you Nicole, you need to get your little self together for the real man God has for you. God is not a magician. You will not see a change overnight. A matter of fact, it takes time. It may take months, maybe years but God doesn't lie about blessing you. When I saw you sitting and talking with Pastor Holcumb, I saw a veil over your head and I saw him in a tuxedo. He is the husband God has for you, but you need to allow him to clean you up. God is a gentleman. He doesn't force himself on us. He waits for us to ask. Nicole, ask. God is ready to give you an extreme makeover," says April.

April jumps up from her seat in the restaurant and starts singing in her Kelly Rowland voice, "Let him be your motivation!"

The people in the restaurant start laughing.

"Sit down crazy. You are so embarrassing! God, help my friend! She has been this crazy since college. How in the world can you go from being a prophetess used by God to singing "Motivation" by Kelly Rowland?" asks Sharon.

Laughing hysterically, Lisa says, "All of you need medication, especially that crazy April! What in the world would I do without any of you?"

"Live a boring life dating married, attached men," laughs Sharon.

"Shut up Sharon. You better be glad I love you because I'd punch you in the face. Ladies, our diversity balances each other. I believe that if one of us lands a husband, it will be a domino effect and we all will," says Lisa.

"Didn't you hear that sermon today, Nicole? It was for you. That's why you started looking crazy at one point. Haha! It's ok. We all live and learn but as your friends, we want to see that low self esteem turn around," says April.

"I am not the only one at this table with issues April. First Lady? All of you are crazy. We had a good conversation while comforting Julie. That is all. I am fat with 3 kids. Good joke, but he doesn't see me like that. I am not first lady material. He was just being nice and cordial," says Nicole.

"I should bust you over your head like Jill Scott did her husband in 'Why Did I Get Married'! Maybe you will get some common sense. One thing God isn't. . . is a joke. I am not playing with you girl, but if you want a **BOTTOMER**, do you boo! I know if God said that a fine man like Pastor Holcumb was my husband, I'd be at his beckoning call saying coffee, tea, me," laughs April.

"It's not easy and none of you understand. I will pray about it," says Nicole.

"This steak is the bomb. Whew! I feel Jesus all up in this loaded baked potato! Whew, this cheese, bacon and sour cream," laughs April as she relishes in her fat girl gone greedy moment.

"What time is it, April? You know we have that evening service to support

Pastor," says Sharon.

"That's right. You know that is Tyrone's church. I want to see what's going on up in there. You know Pastor Holcumb is crazy. If the sister girls and boys are up in there strong, he will put everything on blast. You remember that church we went to with the ministry in DC. Babies, we were gone midway through praise and worship. Elton John was the musician and RuPaul was the Praise and Worship leader. That mess was crazy. We laughed for days," laughs April.

"Yes, I remember because Pastor Simone got in trouble for that engagement. In our leadership meeting, he changed the rules for engagements. Now, the requesting church must send a DVD of a service before Pastor will accept. He tore her tail up over that one. I was in shock. I have never seen him so angry. He gave his famous integrity speech. Instead of trying to be Barbie in a dream house trying to land Ken, she needs to pray and ask God to lead her steps more. The crazy part is that she can **PREACH!!!** She can tear a church up. Her flesh is just out of control like most saved women. We want what we want and there is no stopping us. Once we put our sights on a man, it's him or the highway whether he acts like he wants us or not. We have no business chasing a man. We have no business exhibiting loneliness. That is not of God. Keep busy, pretty, and in shape. In time, if we are supposed to get married, he will show up," says Sharon.

"On a lighter note, this has got be a sin cause this bread is better than a hard one right now," laughs April.

"Take your medicine! You don't know what to say out your mouth," laughs

Sharon.

"We must get out here. It is getting late," says Sharon.

"Waiter, can we get the check and 4 boxes please," says Lisa.

"This has been another wonderful outing as usual. We must all get together again soon," says Sharon.

"I agree," says Lisa.

The check comes and Lisa says, "I got it!"

"Thanks Lady Warbucks," yells April.

"Girl, you are so crazy!" laughs Lisa.

Everyone thanks Lisa and they depart the restaurant.

Buzzz. Buzzzz. . . ..

Lisa receives a text from Lester.

*Babe? – text from Lester*
*Yes? – text from Lisa to Lester*
*I am on my way to your house. Can I hit that just one more time for old times sake? – text from Lester*
*What? – text from Lisa to Lester*

*You know you want it. Don't fight it. I will be at your house waiting. – text from Lester*

*Ok – text from Lisa to Lester*

# STAY TUNED FOR BOOK 2 FEATURING THE LIFE AND TIMES OF APRIL!

# ACKNOWLEDGEMENTS

First of all, I have to thank the Lord Jesus Christ for the ability to express myself in this format. Through my mistakes, failures, and trials, God never gave up on me and kept nudging until I started this path.

Gladys Olivia Mintz, my grandma, I love and miss you everyday. I wish you were here to see me walk into destiny but I know God has allowed you to see that your prayers have paid off. I live to make you and my Mother proud. To know you two are proud makes me feel very overjoyed. Until I see you later, I love you and can you please leave that recipe for the homemade 3 layer chocolate cake that you would make for my birthday on my table. Thank you! (smiling)

Pearlene Mintz (Aunt Bootsie AKA My second mom) has always been a strong example in my life. Your walk of faith is undeniable. Your ability to serve is commendable. I love you!

Hazel Hopewell, my godmother, is the strongest woman I know. And undoubtedly, I know I am the craziest godchild she has. I have shared things with you that I never shared with my mother. I love you with my whole heart and don't ever forget it.

Tiara, Brandon, and Joshua … My babies! Whew! You all keep me praying! I love you and I am determined you will be my greatest accomplishments in life, willingly or unwillingly.

Erica Hall, I am so thankful and grateful that God saw fit to place me in your life as you spiritual mother. I love you! Anytime, you can deal with my craziness then I know you are special. I am not a gift to you, but you are a gift to me. Eyes have not seen and ears have not heard......

Pastor Calvin and First Lady Marion Thomas, I love you too. I questioned the heck out of you as a child. I was inquisitive. It has paid off. You laid my foundation. I attended Sunday School, ushered, counted money, prayed, presided over services, sang in the choir … did everything imaginable in a church under your leadership. You taught me church protocol and I am very grateful.

Apostle Franklin Cornelius Showell & First Lady Augusta Showell, I love you both! I still hear the words of wisdom you have spoken into my life when I am in a dark place. Your teachings of spiritual warfare have prepared me mightily for ministry. You, both, are a true example of kingdom royalty.

Elder Gerald Larts, my brother directly sent from God, Bishop Preston Toogood, the greatest supporter, Overseer Edwin and Yvonne Wither-spoon, Lavel Jones, "Ms. Kind Heart", Garry Sr & Yvonne Green, another set of parents, I love all of you. All of you have spoken words into my life that have changed my life dramatically. You are all special and thank you!

Dr. Todd Hall, I love you! From 1999 to present, God has used you to speak life to these dry bones many, many days. Even though that one "p" word still is unnerving. (smiling). Many times, I would say "If I could only get to a Todd Hall service, I know I will be okay" and you would show up! Thus, I continue to be a-ok. Man looks at the outward. I see the spirit. Enough said. (insider) At this point in life, you are my Pastor until death do us part!

Last, but not least, my road dawg, my BFF, my bestie, my sister, Supreina Mason, I love you. What had happened was God knew one set of parents couldn't handle two off-the-hook, tell it like it, strong, beautiful, pretty daughters so he had to split us up and give us to separate parents. That's my story and I am sticking to it. God always knew I wanted a big sister and he granted my wish 25 years later. Your words of wisdom, constant nagging, and pushing has gotten me to this point and I will be forever grateful.

To those that used me, broke my heart, and spoke ill-will of me just because, thank you! Your abuse and misuse of words keeps me going higher. Without your constant reminder that I wouldn't, couldn't and shouldn't be "her" has catapulted me to being "her". The best part is I haven't completed the transition yet, so watch out now!!

Ana and Shaun Saunders, what can I say? You two have given my vision life. You two are simply amazing. I am thankful that God saw fit to place you in my life to help my vision come to pass. I love you both and YOU ROCK!